EBURY PRESS

SWIPE RIGHT TO KILL

Anirban Bhattacharyya wears many hats. He is a bestselling author, television content producer, stand-up comedian, motivational speaker and an actor. He is the creator, producer, director and writer of the hit true crime TV show *Savdhaan India*. He is also the producer of the hit series *Crime Patrol* and *Fear Files*.

Anirban is the bestselling author of the true crime books *India's Money Heist: The Chelembra Bank Robbery*, launched by superstar Mohanlal and endorsed by S. Hussain Zaidi, and *The Deadly Dozen: India's Most Notorious Serial Killers*, endorsed by John Abraham and Ayushmann Khurrana and launched by Anurag Kashyap.

Anirban likes writing across multiple genres and has written the children's book *The Adventurous 6: The Sinister Summer Holiday*. His previous book *The Hills Are Burning* is a bestselling memoir of his growing-up years in boarding school at Kalimpong amidst the violence of the Gorkhaland agitation in the late 1980s. The book has been hailed as one of the 'boldest' books to shed truth about the Gorkhaland Revolution.

He has been the content head at Channel (V) and the Walt Disney Company (India). He has acted in movies like *Sui Dhaaga* (2018), *Mission Mangal* (2019), *Opium* (2022), *The Broken News* (2022) and more.

Anirban went on to do his bachelor's degree in English literature from St Xavier's College, Kolkata, and a master's degree in film, television and mass communication from A.J.K. Mass Communication Research Centre, Jamia Millia Islamia, New Delhi.

Follow him on http://www.linktr.ee/anirbanb

SWIPE RIGHT TO KILL

TO KILL

THE JAIPUR TINDER MURDER CASE

ANIRBAN BHATTACHARYYA

EBURY
PRESS

An imprint of Penguin Random House

EBURY PRESS

Ebury Press is an imprint of the Penguin Random House group of companies
whose addresses can be found at global.penguinrandomhouse.com

Published by Penguin Random House India Pvt. Ltd
4th Floor, Capital Tower 1, MG Road,
Gurugram 122 002, Haryana, India

Penguin
Random House
India

First published in Ebury Press by Penguin Random House India 2024

ISBN 9780143463665

Typeset in Garamond by MAP Systems, Bengaluru, India
Printed at Thomson Press India Ltd, New Delhi

www.penguin.co.in

MIX
Paper | Supporting
responsible forestry
FSC® C010615

Thanks to SHO Gur Bhoopendra Singh and the Rajasthan Police for allowing this story to be shared with the world, so that people do not make similar mistakes

'The devil's finest trick is to persuade you that he does not exist'
—Charles Baudelaire, *Paris Spleen*

Contents

Author's Note   xi

Chapter One: The Set-Up   1

Chapter Two: Priya Seth: Learning to Fly   13

Chapter Three: Dikshant Kamra: Chasing Dreams   17

Chapter Four: Dushyant: Sincerely Yours   22

Chapter Five: Priya the Femme Fatale   27

Chapter Six: Vivan–Priya–Dikshant   40

Chapter Seven: The Kidnapping   50

Chapter Eight: The Twist   56

Chapter Nine: What Next?   62

Chapter Ten: The Ransom Call   70

Chapter Eleven: The First Step   78

Chapter Twelve: The Murder   85

Chapter Thirteen: The Cover-Up   93

Chapter Fourteen: The Disposal of the Body   99

Chapter Fifteen: The Body Is Discovered   108

Chapter Sixteen: The Morning After   115

Chapter Seventeen: The Evidence Collection   126

Chapter Eighteen: The Interview That
                   Shocked the World   141

Chapter Nineteen: The Diva   157

Afterword   167

Acknowledgements   181

Notes   185

Author's Note

If you are not familiar with this case, here is the starter kit.

On 2 May 2018, Dushyant Sharma, a twenty-eight-year-old man, goes missing. The next morning his family receives a ransom call. They make a partial payment initially, promising to arrange the balance amount.

On the same day, the body of a man is discovered, packed in a trolley bag in Jaipur. The person has been stabbed multiple times. The body is identified to be that of Dushyant Sharma.

With only a bag, a phone call and a body as clues, the Rajasthan Police used their investigative skills and sheer presence of mind to unravel one of the most shocking crimes of India.

The murder was the culmination of years of devious crimes being committed on social media and dating sites.

And more startling was the revelation of the mastermind behind it all—a woman named Priya Seth.

This is the true story of the Jaipur Tinder Murder Case.

(P.S.: Some of the victims' names have been changed for confidentiality purposes.)

Chapter One

The Set-Up[*]

Jaipur. 2016.

It was 7.10 p.m. A Thursday. Winter was slowly on its way out. The financial year ending was around the corner, and Paritosh (a fictional character, who is a combination of Priya's numerous victims) knew that he had tons of work on his hands. Being a chartered accountant, he was already swamped with account closings, filing taxes and trying to adjust the incomes of individuals so that they could find the taxation loopholes and pay lower taxes.

But here he was, seated in his car with the windows rolled up, outside in the parking lot of a two-star hotel, near Jawahar Circle. On the hotel website were photographs of a gym, suites with gold-coloured curtains and upholstery, and

---

[*] This chapter is a fictional representational account based on the reports in various articles, including: Santosh Trivedi, 'वेश्यावृत्ति से जुड़ी साइट्स पर अपना मोबाइल नम्बर छोड़ देती थी प्रिया सेठ, रकम लेती और भाग जाती' (Priya Seth used to leave her mobile number on prostitution related sites, take the money and run away), Patrika, 5 May 2018, https://www.patrika.com/jaipur-news/dushyant-sharma-murder-know-all-about-priya-seth-2754865. This is to introduce the modus operandi used by Priya Seth to the readers.

a restaurant that served 'Chines', 'Muglai' and 'Contynentel' cuisine, spelling be damned, even if it truly was a multi-cuisine restaurant.

Paritosh had made the booking for a room from his phone a few hours ago, when his plan came into fruition. And here he was waiting for the other person to turn up— the other occupant of the room. The one who had promised to show him a good time.

Back in Ajmer, Paritosh had a wife. They were married for sixteen years. They had even been blessed with a son thirteen years ago. He had learnt to love his wife, as their marriage had been an arranged one. His life was routine. Wake up – have breakfast – drop his son to school – office – lunch – meetings – clients – return home – dinner – sleep or sometimes he had sex with his wife, which did not last beyond three minutes (disrobing not included).

In the darkness of the night, he would watch porn on his phone to get aroused. He would then slowly roll over to his wife's side of the bed. He would get close to her, then grind into her back as a pre-mating signal, till she understood what he wanted. She would turn around and he would mount her and exhaust himself. After that, he would roll back to his side of the bed and fall asleep. He rued the fact that she wasn't more participative and that she wasn't able to fulfill his sexual fantasies. Paritosh had to visualize in his head the various porn stars he had seen; the various positions that they indulged in. But in the end, he had to be content with the missionary.

It was mechanical. It was boring. She was no longer young. Her breasts now hung loose after having nursed their son for two years. He conveniently ignored his own gigantic paunch and man-boobs that had developed due to age and his sedentary lifestyle. Paritosh convinced himself mentally that he needed some inspiration to break away from his routine, to get back the mojo in his life.

He needed some R&R. He dreamed of an encounter with someone who was younger, prettier, someone who would help him relive the fantasies that buzzed inside his head. But would it be possible? Added to this were the whiffs of fear and the stench of middle-class moralities.

His younger colleague at the office, Santanu (a fictional character), boasted about his single life to Paritosh. Santanu, it seemed, was having the time of his life in Ajmer, having shifted here from Jabalpur, Madhya Pradesh, far from the overbearing attention of his mother.

'We are only two-and-a-half hours away from a great life. The party is happening in Jaipur!' Santanu had said excitedly.

'Is that why you've chosen to remain single even at thirty-five?' Paritosh said with a tinge of regret in his voice.

'Single, ready to mingle and tingle!' Santanu laughed at his own cheap joke and then continued. 'Look at you at forty-two. You are still young and yet you behave like the world has come to an end for you.'

This was true. Paritosh would listen with regret every time Santanu shared his 'adventures'. Every Monday, Santanu would talk about the young college girls he had hooked up with over the weekend. Santanu would apparently head off to Jaipur on Saturday for his dates and often spend the weekend there. He would return to Ajmer on the Udaipur City Intercity Express 12992 boarding at Jaipur at 2.30 p.m. and hitting home turf two hours later.

'It is so easy. ONS. NSA,' he had told Paritosh, who had looked at him quizzically.

Santanu laughed. 'Get with the lingo, or else they will call you Uncle! ONS is One Night Stand and NSA is No Strings Attached.'

Paritosh could not believe what he was hearing. 'You mean, young girls are willing to just have sex with older men?'

'Of course! They don't want to date just one man. Boss, they want to enjoy life.' Santanu paused for a beat, and continued, 'But obviously, it comes with a price.'

Paritosh was hanging on to every word that Santanu was saying.

'They charge a fee for their time. Every girl charges differently; you know, based on their looks and age. A hot college girl obviously knows that she is hot so she treats herself as premium.'

'*Lekin*, this is like prostitution, right?' Paritosh's middle-class moralities kicked in.

'Sir, these days it is known as escorting. They are escorts who will spend time with you for money. It's companionship for a few hours. And you will obviously pay them for their "services", no?' Santanu emphasized the word 'services', air quoting for good measure.

Paritosh's mind was buzzing. He could feel his loins stirring with the thoughts of impending possibilities. The words 'escort' and 'service' seemed to have quelled his doubts. After all, they would indeed be providing a service. And his fantasy was slowly coming together.

He had three more questions.

'How do I meet these . . . these . . .' he hesitated, searching for the right word, but he settled on the safe, 'girls?'

Santanu took out his mobile phone. It had a crack running down the length of the large screen. He roused it from its slumber and clicked open an app.

'This is Tinder,' he said in a hushed tone, lest someone else get to know about his Ali Baba's cave of endless bounty.

'How does it work?' Paritosh pulled his chair closer to Santanu. On the screen was a beautiful girl with the caption 'Sonal, 22'.

'Have you ever seen a website called Hot or Not from your time?' Santanu's query was met with a blank stare. The silence was the answer.

'Never mind. You see this photo? You can click on the photo to see her profile and read about her. If you like her, you swipe right on the screen. If you don't like her, swipe left.'

'But if I swipe left, will she come to know?' Paritosh did not want to offend the ladies.

'It is anonymous. Only when you swipe right will the woman get an alert and your profile will be visible to her,' Santanu had the smile of an all-knowing sage on his face. He continued, 'And if she too likes you, she will swipe right, and that will be a match. You can then chat with each other and take it forward.'

'So the man has to swipe first?' Santanu's throat felt parched with growing excitement.

'No. Even the woman can "swipe and choose" the man. And if both of you swipe and choose each other, it's fun time! Download the app and create your profile. Remember, you have to make your profile attractive. It is all about looking good. Only then will the hot girls find you attractive. Best of luck!' And there endeth Santanu's lesson.

'And what about the police? This is illegal, no?' Paritosh's libido had entered the house of sin, while his courage, or the lack of it, was holding him back.

'*Jab ladka-ladki razi, tab kya karega qazi?*' (When the boy and girl are ready for marriage, why should the magistrate interfere?) Santanu leaned on the adage.

Paritosh stared at his phone. On the screen were various dating apps that had popped up when he had typed in the input 'Tinder' in the search bar of the app play store.

The word 'tinder' was red in colour and written all in lowercase letters. There was something stylish about the way all the letters had rounded corners. And instead of the dot above the 'I', there was a flame with two tongues reaching upwards, perhaps to symbolize that the contents of the site were indeed 'hot' and not staid and boring.

There was a beat. Paritosh's index finger shakily hovered above the Install button, displayed on his phone screen. And then boom . . . he clicked on it. The download began. And step-by-step, the door to a forbidden world began slowly creaking open for him . . .

He set up his profile. When it came to choosing his name, he could not figure out what to call himself. In the end, he chose Raj.

While investigating another story for my television show *Savdhaan India*, I came to know that the other popular fake names used on social media were Vijay, Ajay, Vinod and Rahul—names that Hindi film scriptwriters have relied on for decades. The logic being that the more common it sounded, the more relatable the audience found the characters on screen. They were popular, mainstream names, devoid of any hint of caste or financial status.

A few years ago, Tinder revealed the list of the most right-swiped names in India. The most popular name for men was Lalit, followed by Joel, Kushagra, Junaid, Ryan, Sandeep, Joshua, Amir, Satya and Michael. While men preferred the name Aanchal when it came to swiping right, followed by Sonal, Kritika, Sakshi, Himani, Sonam, Natasha, Sanjana, Shivani and Isha.[1]

Paritosh lied about his marital status. He couldn't lie about his age considering his rapidly receding hairline. He also wrote about his love for adventure sports and travel, both of which he detested. He accepted the terms and conditions and nervously smiled to himself.

When he logged on and swiped through the photos, he couldn't believe his eyes. Here was a bevy of beauties waiting to be seduced and loved. He remembered Santanu's lesson, 'Not all the women are there for hook-ups. Usually the ugly, ordinary ones are the women looking for love and marriage, having failed to find it in the real world. The hot ones are looking for sugar daddies or hook-ups with money involved.'

'What is a sugar daddy? And how do you know so much?' Paritosh was amazed at the knowledge his colleague had. He was almost on the verge of asking him whether it was a course he studied in college.

'Sugar daddy . . . is like a sponsor . . . a friend with benefits . . . young girl with an older man as a lover. No commitments. The man buys things for her in exchange for sex and companionship,' Santanu explained and then took a long sip from his beer. They were seated at The Rock, one of Jaipur's oldest bars. Like middle-aged, middle-class corporate workers, they had chosen the restaurant as it served a bottle of beer at Rs 99 throughout the whole year.

A burp followed and Santanu continued, 'You see, it is simple logic. Why would the pretty girls and handsome guys come online to search for love? They can easily get hundreds of men and women swooning over them in the real world. So they have ulterior motives for coming on to Tinder. As for the ordinary-looking ones, the simple ones, you can make them out from their profile picture itself. They are desperate—some of them in their forties, especially the women who come to Tinder as a last resort as there is pressure on them to get married. No parents are involved. The prospective bride and groom have taken the onus upon themselves out of desperation.'

Paritosh listened slack-jawed in admiration, hanging on to each word that popped out of Santanu's mouth like pearls of wisdom.

'But what happens if I like a girl from Lucknow and she likes me? Will I have to travel all the way there?' Paritosh was at sea, floundering.

'No!' Santanu shook his head and then pointed to the screen, 'See this slider. It says Maximum Distance. You can set the radius for your search. Other users who are within the radius will appear. So set it to 30kms.'

Paritosh set the 'Distance Preference' to 30 km, and the age preference to twenty-two to twenty-seven.

And it was late December 2016 when he came upon the photo of . . .

Neha,[2] 25. *(The age was perfect. She looked young!)*

8.5 km away. *(So near and yet so far!)*

But he couldn't make out what kind of girl Neha was. She wasn't pretty or hot, neither did she look ordinary or from a middle-class family. So was she looking for a serious relationship or just good old 'adventure'? There was something about her eyes. It seemed to burn through the mobile screen.

Alluring? Perhaps not.

Mysterious? Definitely.

And that half-smile which curved at the corner of her lips excited Paritosh. He hesitated for a beat. And then he swiped right. It felt liberating, like a weight had been lifted off his shoulder. He sat up and began swiping left (reject), right (approved) and centre (super-like).

* * *

Neha Seth[3] was browsing through Tinder when she stopped on the picture of Raj, forty. He was single, loved adventure sports and travelling.

She smiled as she pictured another man walking right into her well-constructed trap. She had been on Tinder for a year now and knew exactly who was trying to hide their identity and who was being honest. She had been born with the unique ability of sussing out people. She knew this was a fake name. People tended to use Shah Rukh Khan's character's name Raj from *DDLJ* quite often. The other popular fake names were Vijay, Ajay, Vinod and Rahul—names that Hindi film scriptwriters had relied on for decades. The logic being that the more common it sounded, the more relatable the audience found the characters on screen. It was a commonplace name devoid of any hint that could give away caste, financial status or even regional provenance.

The guy in the picture was desperately trying to look cool and attractive. Priya swiped right, casting her net into the Tinder sea. Immediately there was a ping—he had matched her as well. A tingling sensation ran down her spine. She knew that 'Raj' was going to be a piece of cake.

* * *

When the first message popped up, Paritosh had been preparing to sleep. The ping made his wife turn around in bed.

'*Phone silence pe kar do*!' (Put your phone on silent mode!) And who's messaging you this late at night?' She was irritated.

Paritosh mumbled something about 'office' and scooted off to the sitting room. He couldn't believe that Neha had replied. For the next two hours, Paritosh was on top of the world as Neha complimented him on his looks and they finalized a date and time to meet to take it 'further'.

'We will meet in the lobby of Hotel XXXX at Jawahar Circle. I will see you at 8 p.m.'[4] was the final instruction given to Paritosh.

* * *

Paritosh checked his watch. It was 7.15 p.m. He got out of the car and headed to the reception of the hotel. Nervous and jumpy, he looked around to ensure no one familiar spotted him. He showed the hotel booking on his mobile screen to the receptionist. The hotel lobby was tiny and smelled of jasmine incense. Behind the receptionist was a flex printout of a painting of a war scene with kings astride elephants and foot soldiers going at each other with spears and swords set against the barren Rajasthan desert landscape.

'No luggage?' the receptionist asked with a smirk. The question made Paritosh uneasy and embarrassed. He mumbled something about only being there for a night. He was led to Room no. 202.

'Why will you be spending the night in Jaipur?' his wife had asked, to which Paritosh made up a cock and bull story about a conference being held there along with an office party.

Paritosh messaged Neha that he had checked in at the hotel and went down to wait for her. At 8.10 p.m., a pretty girl walked into the lobby. Paritosh instantly recognized her from her profile picture on Tinder. There stood Neha.

Paritosh was excited and yet felt nervous like any other man who was on his way to cheat on his wife for the first time. They shook hands and sat down on two chairs in the corner of the lobby, their backs towards the reception.

The first words were spoken by Neha. 'Before we start, can I get the payment?'

Paritosh was a little taken aback by her brusqueness.

'A lot of people don't pay up after they have . . .' She let the silence hang there hoping he would grab it.

'Oh yes! No problem . . . Yes . . . I understand.' He reached into his trouser pocket and withdrew a bundle of notes and handed it over.

'Rs 25,000?'[5] she asked and then proceeded to count the notes. When she was satisfied, she stood up.

'Why don't you go up to the room and get ready while I quickly go and give this to my driver? He is in need of some money. I'll be back in five minutes, and then we can . . .' saying this Neha stepped out of the hotel lobby.

Paritosh ordered a bottle of wine. He waited for five minutes . . . fifteen minutes . . . an hour . . . Neha was nowhere to be seen. He opened his Tinder, wanting to message her, but her profile had vanished. That is when realization hit him: he had been played.

He sat down clutching his head in his hands. He had thrown away almost a month's salary in the hopes of a good night.

Neha aka Priya Seth had walked away from yet another successful mission—punishing a philandering married man who deserved to be taught a lesson. The set up, the long con played over a month and the final lunge had hit the bull's eye.

Paritosh thought for an instant to lodge a complaint at the local police station but withdrew his thoughts immediately. It would expose his failed attempt at seeking pleasure outside of his marriage. That would be devastating! What would people say? He felt like crying, but no tears came.

* * *

What you are about to read is the incredible true story of a woman who conned a thousand men and ended stuffing one into a trolley bag.

This is Priya Seth, who would earn herself the moniker of 'The Tinder Killer'.

Chapter Two

Priya Seth: Learning to Fly

Priya Seth had scored 90 per cent in her 10th board exams and 85 per cent in her 12th. Her father, who was a college professor of political science at a government college in Pali, could not have been prouder of his daughter.[6]

For a middle-class family in a small town in Rajasthan called Falna, education was the only way to get out of this place that boasted a nineteenth-century Jain temple and a population of 25,000 people.

Located 29 km from Falna are the famous granite Jawai Hills that is home to sixty-odd leopards that incredulously roam freely amongst the human population there, without attacking them. The leopards helped Falna get footfalls as the tourists used the town for passing through to the hills.

Unbeknownst to Ashok Seth, or Professor *saab*, his daughter would, in just a few years, turn into a ruthless hunter preying on the innocent, in her own version of the jungle adage 'survival of the fittest'. And this would put Falna across news channels of the country, for all the wrong reasons!

When Priya was in school, her father would often show off the achievements of his gifted daughter to their friends, relatives and neighbours, pointing at the shelves lined with numerous medals and certificates that Priya had won during her school years, 'We are soon going to run out of space on these shelves!' There would be a twinkle in his eye, and his chest would swell with pride. Priya was talented not only in her studies but also in dancing and debating. But as she grew older, the talented and happy child began displaying hints of the growing darkness inside her like a virus that would soon consume her completely.

Priya had an issue. She was stubborn and was prone to angry outbursts when she didn't get what she wanted. Her parents were used to these outbursts. Her indulgent father labelled her as being merely 'stubborn'.

Post Priya's arrest, her father spoke to journalist Snigdha Poonam and reminisced saying, '[She was] good at dance, debating. Our shelves are lined with her medals and certificates. You can't tell this seeing her in jail, but she used to be so beautiful.' She was also problematic. 'Stubborn. What she wanted, she wanted. Got angry easily. Broke things at home. Couldn't take no. Didn't have the fear of anything.'[7]

Priya, on her part, felt trapped in Falna. She saw no future for herself in the town.

She was confined in her miserable and ordinary life. She knew as soon as she finished college, her parents would bring up the dreaded topic of 'settling down' and marriage. Predictably, this would be followed by the expectations of delivering children like a well-oiled machine.

Priya was determined to not let her parents chop through her tapestry of dreams. She was aware that the movie in her head was much larger than what the town of Falna could offer her.

In 2012, Priya left for Jaipur. She enrolled at Parishkar College to study arts while simultaneously taking coaching classes to prepare for the entrance exam of the Indian Administration Service.

Falna is almost equidistant from Kota and Jaipur. Kota is known for its rigorous coaching centres that train lakhs of civil service aspirants every year, so much so that it has earned the dubious moniker of 'Kota Factory'. But Priya's parents chose the flashier city of Jaipur instead for her.

As soon as Priya landed in Jaipur, the city welcomed her, showing off its brightest lights and loudest life. She loved Jaipur. Falna was no patch on the glitzy and fast Jaipur. Priya instantly knew she wouldn't be going back to Falna again.

Sliding doors: what if Priya had chosen to go to studious Kota instead of the faster and glitzier Jaipur? Would her life have turned out to be different?

Priya, the small-town girl, was initially shy and a little reluctant. When she saw her classmates at college, she felt her clothes weren't fashionable enough; she was embarrassed. Her shoes looked ordinary. Her classmates wore fashionable sleeveless tops, the latest pair of jeans and trendy shoes. Some of them wore branded clothes and they all smelled so nice wearing their imported perfumes. Priya felt out of place.

Priya had been the cynosure of all eyes at Falna, where people always praised her for her talent. In Jaipur, no one gave her a second look. From being a large fish in a small pond, she suddenly had become a tiny fish in a gigantic ocean. She had come from a small town and was seen as an outsider who was not as 'cool' as her Jaipur classmates. She was also not rich, someone who could afford to hang out at expensive restaurants, clubs or coffee shops along with the 'happening' crowd.

This scarcity of money also meant she could not afford to 'buy' this new lifestyle. She lacked both class and money.

Priya realized that while she lacked these 'essentials', she could turn her life around by making money—lots of it, so that she could have the life she aspired for.

Every month, her father would send her Rs 20,000[8] for her room rent, tuition fees and food. But this was never enough for her. Priya had already succumbed to the temptation of living an extravagant life. She wanted to have the lifestyle of her affluent classmates, though she did not have the means.

Priya Seth made up her mind. Jaipur was going to be the city where she would earn her fortunes. She loved the city but hated the people who made her feel inadequate and like an outsider. She was determined to make Jaipur and its people love her back. She was going to be rich.

She had immense confidence, matched by her lack of fear of anything or anyone, fuelled by her stubborn determination to make it, so that she could rise above her mediocre, middle-class existence.

Unbeknownst to Priya, her destiny was about to get intertwined with somebody else's. And that would be the reason for one of the most heinous crimes the country has seen.

Chapter Three

Dikshant Kamra: Chasing Dreams

Priya Seth and Dikshant Kamra—they were like two moths drawn to the bright flame of glamour and glitz and fated to be ultimately consumed by it. And so they came together like Bonnie and Clyde or the fictional Mickey and Malorie (Oliver Stone's *Natural Born Killers*). It was destiny that two souls from nowhere crashed into each other and destroyed not only their own lives but also took another's.

Sri Ganganagar in Rajasthan is a city near the international border of India and Pakistan, named after Maharaja Shri Ganga Singh Bahadur, Maharaja of Bikaner, who established it. It is located at the point where the fertile waters of the River Sutlej enter into Rajasthan. The Maharaja meticulously planned the layout of Ganganagar, dividing it into residential blocks and commercial areas, just like he had seen in Paris.

And just 39 km from the well-planned and well-connected city of Ganganagar lies Padampur. A city that has no direct railway link to the rest of the country. The nearest railway station is 20 km away at Gajsinghpur. The city is so nondescript that a Google search of 'Padampur Rajasthan' throws up two commonplace and random pictures of a white horse and a four-point road!

The city was named after Rajkumar Padam Singh of the royal family of Bikaner.

And it is here, in Padampur, that Dikshant Kamra aka Rocky was born.

Since childhood, he aspired for a life that was beyond the grasp of his middle-class parents. His father, Rajeev Kamra, was a schoolteacher (just like Priya's) who like almost all Indian parents had already chalked out the life and career of his son the moment he took his first breath. But Dikshant was not happy with that plan. He wanted to have control of his life and that led to differences between him and his parents, particularly his father.

His sounding board for his frustrations was his classmate, Lakshya Walia.

'I need to get out of here . . .' Dikshant complained to Lakshya. Both of them were in Class X, and they had their life, full of promise and opportunities, ahead of them. They were the architects who stood at the brink of designing their own lives.

Dikshant wanted to head to Delhi and Mumbai. When his friend Lakshya asked him what he would do there, Dikshant replied that he wanted to be a model.

Dikshant's schoolteacher-father Rajeev Kamra was not at all pleased when he came to know that his son wanted to do modeling, a profession that did not figure in his traditional book of stable career options. He wanted his son to complete his college education and at least get a degree.

But Dikshant had made up his mind. So after his Class X exams, he made his way to New Delhi to try his hand in modelling. But luck evaded him.

'If you want to be a model, you are in the wrong city, bro! Mumbai is the place to be,' someone advised him. And Dikshant packed his bags once again in search of glamour, fame and money.

In Mumbai, Dikshant joined the throng of struggling models and actors who come to the city with dreams in their eyes and hope in their hearts but soon realize that the soles of their shoes cannot outlast their struggles to fulfill aspirations and their dreams.

In order to pay his rent, he started working in films and television serials in whatever capacity he could. When Gur Bhoopendra Singh, the station house officer (SHO) of Jhotwara Police Station (Jaipur), first met Dikshant after his arrest, he knew there was more to him than meets the eye.

'Dikshant lived in Mumbai for two to two and a half years and I think he is not telling us clearly what he used to do there. He says he used to work in films and television serials, but considering his pricey clothes and accessories, we suspect he was involved in some illegal business.'[9]

He continued modelling in Mumbai and dreamt of the one big break that would change his life forever. In the world of struggle and showbiz, it is all about *jo dikhta hai, woh bikta hai*' (What is seen creates an impact / gets sold). The image is more important than the reality. So to keep his head above the other wannabes, Dikshant had an expensive lifestyle that included wearing branded clothes and shoes, staying in hotels and hanging out at fancy restaurants.

When the acting roles were not rolling in, Dikshant decided to try his hand at becoming a producer for an assignment. What he did not anticipate was the difference of being an actor, where he had to just remember his lines and perform, being a producer. Suddenly, the burden and responsibility of funding a project, managing the shoot, the payments to vendors, ensuring that the project comes within the specified budget, all piled up on Dikshant's shoulders. This was new to him, and he drowned not knowing how to swim in this new sea. Shit hit the fan! Dikshant faced a loss of approximately Rs 25 lakh. The creditors began calling him up. Dikshant had no other option but to jump ship and escape from Mumbai to the place where he could be safe—Jaipur.

In March 2018, Dikshant scurried back to Jaipur and met up with his childhood friend and classmate Lakshya Walia and started staying with him at a rented flat in Nandpuri. By this time, Dikshant had lost his father and his widowed mother continued to live in Sri Ganganagar. Dikshant wanted to start a new life. He thought running away from Mumbai would get the creditors off his back. Little did he know that while he may have escaped the wrath of the people he owed money to, fate had ensnared him in a cruel, twisted game that would soon change his life forever.

Events in life may appear as random or at best coincidental. The decisions that we take may seem to be independently done without any interference or influence, but everything in life has been chalked out for us—every step, every decision. We are just bots playing out our roles in The God Edition of The Sims.

Lakshya Walia was at the wrong place at the wrong time. The mistake that got him embroiled in this mess was his greed for money, liquor and fun.

Lakshya and Dikshant were school friends at Sri Ganganagar. And when Dikshant left for Delhi after his Class X results, Lakshya suddenly found himself alone. The fun was sucked out of his life as his family now put pressure on him to start working. It was then that Lakshya came to Jaipur to pursue his Bachelor of Business Administration (BBA) and began living at Tanishq Apartment, Nandpuri. When Dikshant turned up in Jaipur in March 2018 and had no place to stay, it was but natural that the childhood friends would live under the same roof. So Dikshant moved into Lakshya's flat at Tanishq Apartment at Nandpuri, Malviya Nagar. Lakshya's life suddenly brightened up and the fun was back.

Chapter Four

Dushyant: Sincerely Yours

'A twenty-five—twenty-six-year-old man doesn't disappear on his own.'
—Dushyant's friend

When Rameshwar Sharma and Vaijanti Sharma got married, they had envisioned a perfect life for themselves. Rameshwar wanted to have children right away. He wanted to give them his youth. The couple prayed devotedly to the gods to grant them male heirs. Their prayers were answered and within a period of ten years they had three sons. While the Sharmas were blessed with male heirs, their perfect life soon turned sour.

Their firstborn died as a child. The other two sons did not know what was going on at that time. They were too young to comprehend death. But it was as if an invisible curse enveloped the Sharma household. While the gods may have answered their prayers initially, they were now in a mood to reclaim them.

As if the death of the first son wasn't a big enough blow, the Sharmas lost their second son in a bike accident, leaving

Dushyant as the lone surviving son, heir, hope and salvation. And Dushyant knew he had to now shoulder the unfulfilled desires, dreams and expectations of his parents. He had to be the ideal son.

One of Rameshwar's favourite moments of the day was to watch his son wake up. Dushyant would offer his prayers as soon as he woke up. He was a devout man. A daily ritual that he followed before retiring for the night was counting his prayer beads.

Vaijanti always worried for her son. She knew he was too straightforward, simple and honest. As she would watch him say his prayers at night, she would pray for his safety too. Sometimes she would gently place his head on her lap and run her fingers through his hair, knowing she would not always be there to protect him.

So she and her husband decided to do the next big thing—to get Dushyant married as soon as possible; their logic being it would teach him to be responsible. They started looking for a suitable wife for their only son. They wanted the best for him.

In 2015, Dushyant got engaged to Bittu. Like a butterfly emerging from a cocoon, Dushyant discarded his shyness to express his unbridled joy on that day. Everyone was stunned to see the new Dushyant go down on his knee and propose to Bittu. His parents were both amused and relieved. They knew they had made the right decision.

After their wedding, Bittu moved into the Sharmas' Shivpuri Extension house. Dushyant was a loving and caring husband—the kind every girl dreams of, and the obedient son that typical Indian parents wish for. He would dress neatly to work, ensuring his hair was well-oiled and parted precisely.

He was respectful of his elders, touching their feet and seeking their blessings when they visited. But he did not have too many friends. He was an introvert. Dushyant was employed in a mining company as a project manager. He maintained regular working hours and he never went out of the house once he came back from work. He was a homebody.

Bittu soon realized how shy her husband was. '[He] never spoke to any of my female friends. He used to hide in our room if they came home. He wasn't interested in *aaj-kal ki ladkiyan* [modern girls],' Bittu revealed in an interview.[10]

Dushyant was not the typical regressive, misogynist and sexist kind who liked to control their wives or who thought that a woman's place is in the kitchen. He never raised his voice or his hand on his wife. What Bittu found most endearing about her husband was that he was passionate about cooking.

'What do you think?' He looked at his wife expectantly as she tasted the kadhai paneer cooked by him. 'It's delicious,' Bittu exclaimed. Dushyant's go-to dishes included hara-bhara kabab, spring rolls and kadhai paneer.[11]

A year and a half into their marriage, in the summer of 2017, Bittu and Dushyant were blessed with a son. Everything was perfect . . . except it was not.

Rameshwar and Vaijanti had no clue that their obedient and *sanskaari* son was leading a double life. Bittu, who was enamoured with her husband's honesty and caring nature, did not get the slightest whiff of who Dushyant was, once he stepped out of the house. While at home, he was a dutiful son, but his online avatar was completely different. It was someone who loved partying, who wore funky tee shirts, gelled hair and cool shades. His social media profile was an anti-thesis of his real self. He led the life of Dr Jekyll and Mr Hyde.

This alter ego was born when he got himself a smartphone. He immediately took to social media and online platforms like fish to water. He frequently ordered food and shopped online as well. He spent a good deal of time scouring through websites too.

On social media, Dushyant was exposed to a life he always dreamt of having but had no access to—the parties, the fun, the women and a carefree life. Dushyant became a pretender. Offline, he pretended to be an ideal son and a caring husband, while online, he pretended to be this cool, rich dude who could afford a lavish life. On Facebook, he appeared like a cool, party-loving boy in printed T-shirts and aviators and with spiked hair.

Why would someone like Dushyant suddenly go rogue? What makes a simple man resort to duplicitous ways? What ignited his carnal desires? Was he bored at home? Did he crave variety? Did he want things that were taboo and forbidden?

The emotion and joy he had once felt with Bittu now seemed distant. And he yearned for a new adventure.

Priya yearned for an aspirational life that was beyond her means. She wanted money, a better lifestyle and access to a world that was beyond her middle-class means.

Dikshant wanted to be an actor. He wanted to be famous, to stand out in the crowd. Just like insects require molting to grow, Dikshant wanted to shed every layer of Sri Ganganagar from his skin.

All three lives were heading towards each other; fated to crash at the crossroads.

Dushyant began to flirt with fire. He did not hesitate to risk his well-balanced and settled domestic life as he stepped into the murky world of online dating. He wanted to have his cake and eat it too. The grass indeed looked greener on the cyber-side.

The virtual world he was part of did not come with responsibilities or accountability. There was freedom from consequences as well as the comfort and convenience of anonymity. He thought he could get away with pretending, having his share of 'fun', deceiving his family.

When the police later pressed Dushyant's colleague for information, one of them squealed, 'Once in a while he had girlfriend scene . . . A 25–26-year-old man doesn't disappear on his own.'[12]

This revealed Dushyant had multiple encounters with women outside his marriage. The adage of *'ek haath se taali nahi bajti'* (you can't clap with one hand) would soon be revealed to Dushyant's parents who had thought him to be innocence personified.

And this is where the 'laws of attraction' kicked in. Here were three people who wanted a life beyond their grasps.

Chapter Five

Priya the Femme Fatale

In the Bollywood film *Bluffmaster!* (Dir: Rohan Sippy, 2005), the eponymous character says, *'Hamare dhande mein na bandook chalti hai, na bomb, na chaku, chalta hai toh sirf ek hi cheez . . . dimaag . . . aur woh hamesha hamare saath rehta hai, loaded.'* (In our business of conning, we don't need guns, bombs or knives, the only thing we need is our brains and that's always ready, loaded.)

Had Priya Seth seen the Abhishek Bachchan-Priyanka Chopra-Nana Patekar starrer? Because she was about to bring her A-Game to the world of conning.

Soon after moving to Jaipur, Priya lost interest in her studies. She was tempted by the lavish lifestyle her classmates had. She knew money was the only gateway. And so while in her second year at Parishkar College, she started looking for a job. She knew her college degree wouldn't be enough to help her secure the kind of life she aspired for.

'The Rs 20,000 that I was sending her every month for her expenses didn't cut it. She wanted to be a crorepati,' her father recalled.[13]

Priya would go on to tell the investigating officer Gur Bhoopendra Singh that she had come for her studies but got lost in the glitz and glamour.

Priya searched newspapers and online sites that offered jobs to freshers. There were jobs for typists (she wasn't professionally trained to be one), for data entry (what is that? she asked) and for office secretary (that could be a start, she thought to herself). But it was an advertisement that said, *'Earn Thousands Easily and Instantly. No Educational Qualifications Required'* that caught her eye.

Priya immediately called up on the number provided and in return was promptly called in for an interview.

This was a gang of pimps who ran escort agencies and prostitution rings. She was offered the job of an escort, with the promise of a bonus if she could recruit young college girls. Priya was initially hesitant. She sat on her decision for days. She wanted the good life, but here she was in a moral dilemma. The pimps were fully aware that the girls who applied for this job were mostly from middle-class homes, desperate for money, and they often employed the pull-push technique to break them down.

They would tempt them with dreams of a lavish lifestyle and immediately follow it up with snarky comments like 'I don't think you are capable of doing it,' 'You look scared,' 'If you don't want to do it, that's fine, we understand.'

This is the same technique that is used to instil peer pressure and the victims end up doing things because they feel the need to prove themselves in front of these doubting Mohans and Neelams.

Priya always got what she wanted. And it was this ego that made her blind even to herself. She stepped into the *boudoir* to offer herself to customers, in her ambition-fuelled craving to reach beyond the stars. She knew this one decision would set in motion larger wheels. She was concentrating on the 'big picture'.

The easy and quick influx of money brought with it a life Priya always dreamt of having. She no longer needed to be dependent on her father financially; she was her own boss. As the extravagant life began to claim her like the ocean claims a shipwreck—bit by bit, corroding it, covering it with weeds—she began copying the affluent girls of her college and their lifestyles. She began to drink and smoke.

One of the newspaper reports quoted the police as saying that Priya 'came in contact with an agent through an advertisement for a part-time job. The agent asked her to rent an apartment that would be used for prostitution and assured her of good money in exchange'.[14]

The police officer, on the condition of anonymity, according to the news report, was quoted as saying, 'She would befriend wealthy people through dating platforms and escort service websites and invite them to her flat. When the men arrived, she would threaten to register a rape case against them if they did not give her money.'[15]

Although Priya denied the above, it is not hard to disbelieve her, considering the refined modus operandi she later used via Tinder.

As the lifestyle and easy money consumed her life, studies took a back seat. She dropped out of college in the second year. Her parents too stopped sending her money as she dropped out of college. Her father was not as angry as he was disappointed. He couldn't believe that his intelligent daughter would drop out of college and waste her life.

Soon, Priya Seth aka Neha Seth became a *'contrepreneur'* and launched her business. On numerous escort-offering websites she promised high-profile, young escorts. Having had 'experience' for two years in this 'sector', she refined her modus operandi.

She targeted middle-aged men.

1. She wanted successful men who were desperate for an 'adventure'. She wanted to exploit this 'need' because that blinded these men, making them gullible.
2. She wanted to target middle-aged men who had careers or were successful. This ensured they would be able to pay up.
3. She knew that most of these middle-aged men would be married and therefore would keep their 'encounter' as confidential, even if they got conned.
4. And the above three immediately sifted out the middle-class variety and the young college boys. As they would find themselves out of the league and in deep waters when it came to the price tag.

According to SHO Singh, dozens of websites offering escort services are created every day, and the police take down close to twenty of them every day. It is a Herculean task to keep track of all these websites and then to follow the mobile numbers advertised on them. And Priya used this cleverly.

Priya left her number on various websites that offered 'escort services in Jaipur'. She limited her services and her clientele to within the city limits of The Pink City. Soon clients started contacting her. When they messaged her on WhatsApp, she sent them photos to choose from. These were of young, attractive college girls. Once the client chose the girl, Priya would request for the entire payment to be made upfront at the rendezvous point, which was usually a hotel booked by the client. The charges would vary according to the kind of girl they chose and the duration the client booked the services for—ranging from an hour to even a day.

Priya would turn up at the luxury hotel, meet the client at the hotel lounge and collect the cash. She had identified a few hotels near Jawahar Circle which she used to suggest to her clients for their rendezvous. Sometimes she would also meet them at public places such as markets and parks or on the streets. Once the money was collected, she would tell the client to go to their hotel room and wait. And then on the pretext of sending the girl, who was supposedly waiting in the parked car or promising to return after securing the cash, she would disappear with the money, switch off her phone and change her mobile number. The client's libidinous plans would end up in a cold shower. 'In these cases, many victims don't turn up due to fear of public humiliation,' says Bhopal Singh, the SHO of Vaishali Nagar Police Station.[16]

Priya would charge Rs 25,000–30,000 on an average and try to con at least four customers in a day. And predictably, no one approached the police for help, or lodged a complaint for fear of exposing their own libidinous liaison. Priya Seth soon became a catfishing queen!

* * *

In 2014, one of Priya's clients called her bluff. He lodged a police complaint and filed a case of cheating against her at the Shyamnagar Police Station in Jaipur.[17] Priya was arrested and booked under the Immoral Traffic (Prevention) Act, 1956. But lo and behold, she was released on bail shortly thereafter. As she was a college-going student (at least on paper), the judge and the cops showed her sympathy. They let her out with an admonishment, much like a stern parent scolding their child. But that same year, she seemed to be in quite a hurry to make money and this time she tried something audacious.

2014 was a watershed year for Priya who was twenty-three at that time. That year, a carpenter by the name of Anil Jangid came to Priya's rented accommodation at Swej Farm Road to fix some furniture. Anil lived in Gajsinghpura's Sundar Nagar locality.[18] They got chatting.

According to the police, what attracted Priya to him was his determination to earn money by any means possible. For Priya, it was like looking at herself in the mirror.

It is here that both of them began discussing their plans to rob an ATM machine. Priya's arrest made her a bit cautious about her 'business'. She stopped conning people for a few months, which led to a drop in her income. She had to maintain the extravagant lifestyle she had gotten used to by now. And this meant that Priya, like a true CEO, had to look for an alternate source of revenue for her company and business. And the ATM heist was just that.

If you ask me, it is impossible to believe that Priya truly fell in love with the man, keeping in mind her social status and the kind of lifestyle she led. I think Anil was just another man she used for her own gain. She duped him into believing that she was in love with him. She used her charm, her body and her shrewd brain to manipulate him to do her bidding.

For the next few days, Priya searched the Internet, gathering as much information as she could about ATM security, how the locks work, how thick the walls of the ATM machine are and also the front panel. She then bought a gas cutter for Rs 10,000 from Sansar Chandra Road. Like criminal masterminds, the duo began doing reconnaissance of various ATM booths and machines. They identified a Bank of India's ATM at Rajat Path in the Mansarovar area.

'At around 3 a.m., both of them went inside the ATM where there was no security guard, smashed the CCTV and started cutting open the ATM. They tore apart one part of the machine entirely and managed to extract a couple of currency notes when two constables on patrol duty—Mahipal Singh and Ankit—came there,' said the investigating officer.[19]

Mahipal and Ankit were both part of the night flying squad. The nights were usually uneventful as they patrolled the streets. But on this occasion, they saw bright sparks and lights coming from inside the ATM booth. This alerted them and they walked over to investigate. Priya had no hesitation leaving her 'boyfriend' behind as she scooted out of the ATM to evade being arrested.

But as the Bollywood dialogue goes: *'Kanoon ke haath lambe hote hain!'* (You can't escape the long arm of the law!) Priya was nabbed three hours later from her friend's house in Mansarovar. The 'boyfriend' had his revenge for being unceremoniously abandoned earlier, by revealing and squealing about her location.

As soon as Priya was brought in and her personal details came to the fore, the police were shocked to find the daughter of a professor who was educated to be involved in such a heist! And soon her records started tumbling out as the police were made aware about Vaishali Nagar Police arresting her previously for prostitution three months ago.[20]

But surprisingly, Priya walked out scot-free just a day later![21] She feigned innocence. She claimed she had been conned and pressurized by Anil to become his accomplice. She pleaded her case as a woman who was waylaid by her own ambition to become economically independent and self-sufficient. Priya had no qualms about playing the 'woman' card. And she definitely was a much better actor than her future-boyfriend Dikshant Kamra.

When she came out, Priya realized that there was no shortcut to the life she wanted. There was not going to be one big haul or a lottery ticket. She had to gather and earn wealth over a period of time. So she buried her head in the sand, like an ostrich, blocking out all the chaos, and went back to her catfishing business. She no longer had to sell her body—all she sold were false promises.

Not only was she 'punishing' the errant men for their philandering ways but also financing her own dreams as well. *Sone pe suhaga!* She had struck gold.

Newspapers would later (after her arrest) report about her extravagant lifestyle, saying, she wore shoes worth Rs 35,000. A designer watch worth Rs 45,000 hung from her wrist. She drank Black Label scotch and Himalayan branded water. Her monthly expenses varied in different newspaper reports. *Dainik Jagran* estimated it to be Rs 2 lakh, while *Rajasthan Patrika* revealed her monthly expenses to be Rs 1.5 lakh.[22]

She could now buy the expensive perfumes, the branded clothes and the foreign cosmetics and travel by air. But her dream was to head to Mumbai to play the big tables, and to earn more money. The glitzy lights of Jaipur now seemed like an old boyfriend she wanted to leave, as he was no longer useful to her.

In 2017, Priya managed to ensnare Gurujar Singh. And this time she even uprooted herself from her hunting ground of Jaipur and shifted to Noida with him. They were in a live-in relationship. Priya was like a parasite, a leech. And Gurujar was one more man who she used, to get access to a lavish lifestyle, which was way beyond her means. But soon, Gurujar realized something was off in the relationship. His girlfriend had too many demands and was high maintenance. And he found her to be too clingy and demanding. Gurujar decided to end the relationship. This came as a shock to Priya. She always envisioned herself to be the epitome of beauty—irresistible and a catch. Inside that tiny head of hers resided a huge psychotic ego.

And so when Gurujar broke the news about the break-up, Priya realized her pipeline of comfort and a good life had been shut off. Her shrewd brain started whirring. She threatened Gurujar with false rape charges.[23]

Priya laid out the detailed plan in her warped head. She knew the law was more empathetic towards women. So her plan was to falsely accuse Gurujar of raping her. The minimum punishment for rape is ten years and this is the scimitar she dangled above his head. The choice was clear: either Gurujar paid her Rs 10 lakh or she would go to the cops and lodge the false case and ruin his life.

Gurujar was not having any of it. He didn't give in. And when that threat did not work, she conjured up a new one, this time a violent one. She threatened to throw acid on Gurujar's sister's face and ruin her life forever if he didn't pay up.[24]

By this time, Gurujar had had enough. All he wanted was to be free from her clutches. So he paid her Rs 4 lakh, hoping she would climb down off his back like the mythical Betaal and disappear.[25] But Priya was greedy and she continued, this time with a brand new threat.

This time, she threatened Gurujar, like a badly scripted and hackneyed 1980s Bollywood movie, saying she was expecting his child. And if he didn't pay her the money, she would announce to the world, and then dump the baby on him. This blackmail and threatening went on for the next two months. Priya was desperate. Unfortunately for Priya, Gurujar by this time had seen through her, and therefore did not fall for her shenanigans.

When you are doing deep-sea fishing with a rod, setting the 'drag' on the line is very important. The drag is a set of two friction plates inside the fishing rod reels that adjusts how much the fish can pull before it simply pulls line off the reel. If the fish pulls on the line hard enough, the friction is overcome, and the reel rotates backwards, letting line out, preventing the line from breaking. So when you have a 200-pound tuna or a big fish on the line, you have to set the drag correctly, lock yourself in a swivel chair or a 'fighting chair' and ensure you don't get pulled overboard.

Priya may have been expert in catfishing, but she was a greedy angler. She had multiple lines in the sea and safety was the last thing on her mind. She was just hoping to get multiple 'bites'. The last thing she expected was *Jaws* to come back for her!

On 23 January 2018, Gurujar Singh registered a case of blackmailing against her with the Vaishali Nagar Police Station. He had had enough of her threats.[26]

Priya was confident she would get away with these threats. Or even if the police did arrest her, she knew she would get away. Except, Jaipur Police was already investigating cases of 'blackmail gangs' that were operating in the city and in Ajmer. Blackmailing and honey trapping men had suddenly become the biggest and easiest business venture. There was minimal investment needed and huge returns.

* * *

On the Christmas Eve of 2016, the Special Operations Group (SOG) of Rajasthan Police arrested a gang that was running one of these blackmail units. The SOG was shocked to learn that the ringleaders were lawyers. Akshat Sharma, Vijay, who is better known as Sonu Sharma, Naveen Devani (lawyer), Anand Shandilya (lawyer) and Nitesh Bandhu Sharma were arrested. Devani and Shandilya were the masterminds behind this extortion ring.[27]

While Devani and Shandilya scoped and identified the targets, who were mostly well-to-do men in local social circles, Akshat, Vijay and several other suspects would traffic girls from Jaipur, Ajmer and also parts of Himachal Pradesh and Uttarakhand.

The plan was simple: the girls would lure the men into making sexual relations with them. This 'encounter' would then be surreptitiously recorded on video. Then the gang members would approach the targets posing as media reporters with the 'evidence' including video clippings and demand hefty hush money ranging from lakhs to crores. If anyone refused to pay up, the lawyers would spring into action and a fake case of rape would be lodged against the targets. And the girls would perfectly play their role of victims, coached by the lawyers. In case the money was paid during the trial, the girls would turn hostile. The gang extorted approximately Rs 15 crore from at least twenty-five people!

The investigation into the gang was based on a complaint by one of the victims, Dr Sunit Soni, who had a hair transplant clinic in Jaipur. When he refused to give in to the blackmail and pay them Rs 1 crore, the gang of lawyers lodged the fake rape case against him. Dr Soni spent the next seventy-five days in jail. The doctor's family eventually paid the money, and predictably the girls turned hostile in the court and denied that they were raped.

The gang would invest the money from the blackmailing in real estate and a lavish lifestyle.[28]

In another case, the SOG arrested Shikha Tiwari aka DJ Adaa, a disc jockey in Mumbai who blackmailed a Jaipur-based individual and ran away with Rs 1 crore.[29]

Then there was the case of Akansha Hizkil, who was part of a larger group of blackmailers. She had managed to blackmail at least fifteen men, falsely accusing them of rape. The SOG arrested her from Ajmer.[30]

In another case, Ravneet Kaur, a non-resident Indian, came to India in 2008 to stay with her grandmother in Haryana's Ambala. She then enrolled herself in a college in Jaipur to study BBA. There, she met a man called Rohit, who was also a student there. Ravneet dropped out of college in the second year (just like Priya) and started looking for a job. Rohit introduced her to Akshat Sharma. Meanwhile, her parents had fixed up her marriage to a Canadian-Indian. She did not want to get married and continued to stay back in Jaipur and Kota. The blackmail gang would use her to extort nearly Rs 4 crore in the next four years. The SOG arrested her as well.[31]

* * *

During this time, two things happened that partially upset Priya's expectations.

First, due to the booming business of honey trap, catfishing and blackmail, the police had become strict, and Priya was seen as a perpetrator, rather than the victim, when she lodged the complaint. The police had smelled the rat.

Second, Priya could never anticipate that there would be someone smarter than her. She suffered from a delusional sense of importance and self-worth. So she thought she could get away. Except, Gurujar had been prepared. Over the months when she harassed, threatened and blackmailed him, Gurujar had recorded his WhatsApp calls with Priya on another phone and presented them to the Vaishali Nagar Police. Gurujar produced the trump card and Priya was left stunned and seething, outwitted at her own game.

In the recordings, Priya's diabolic nature and her desperation to extract money from Gurujar were revealed. Her constant portrayal of herself as the innocent victim to the outside world was now exposed and in tatters. The police were now privy to Gurujar's audio recordings, in which Priya could be heard screaming and threatening to throw acid on Gurujar's sister's face if he did not cough up the money. And 'I will upload your sister's photo on escort websites. I will kill you and your family. I will destroy your life.'

Gurujar presented all the evidence to SHO Bhopal Singh and Inspector Nidhi Dhaka at the Vaishali Nagar Police Station.

The drama was just beginning . . .

Chapter Six

Vivan–Priya–Dikshant

It was in October 2017 that Dushyant stumbled upon Tinder. He just couldn't get his eyes off the app. Disbelief, incredulity and lasciviousness, all rolled into one, permeated through his senses. So many available women, at his fingertips. On Facebook, he was already the stylish, cool dude, which was a complete anti-thesis to his drab real life. And this extrovert alter ego is what he transposed from Facebook to Tinder.

The comfort of anonymity gave him the chutzpah to adopt a new identity. He knew that in order to be successful in 'picking up' girls, he needed to come across as chase-worthy and aspirational. And thus was born Vivan Kohli, in this new parallel timeline and multiverse. Vivan was this wealthy businessman from New Delhi, with assets running into millions. And most importantly, he was single and available.

Dushyant's family had no clue what was going on. His parents thought of him as the God-fearing person, someone who loved his family. His wife Bittu was stuck in the house playing mother, babysitter, wife and daughter-in-law.

She believed her husband to be of sound moral principles and ethics. Except, he wasn't.

In February 2018, Destiny played her hands with a cackle, as she already knew the outcome. The others around the table—Luck and Fate—stared at Destiny wondering why she was so happy. Destiny just smiled and said, *'Picture toh abhi shuru hui hai!'* (The movie has just started!)

February 2018. Priya had been swiping away on Tinder when she came across the profile of Vivan Kohli, a rich businessman from New Delhi who visited Jaipur quite often. Two things caught her eye: rich and New Delhi. These two ticked off the necessary boxes for her modus operandi.

Priya met Dushyant a couple of times at cafés. Dushyant had to plan these rendezvous meticulously so as to not raise suspicions at home. And so he would take off early from work. A couple of his colleagues deciphered the spring in his steps and realized that Dushyant had a 'girlfriend scene'.

For the first time, Priya Seth changed her modus operandi.

What did she sense in Dushyant? She did not 'offer' him other girls but stepped on to the court herself. She did not lure him to a hotel room and siphon off his money like she usually did with her Tinder catches.

The answer is Priya aka Neha Seth seeing Vivan to be a rich businessman, probably looked at him to be the goose that would lay the golden eggs for her every week, just like her ex-boyfriend Gurujar. She used the long con method for him.

She went all out to convince him that she loved him, because she thought he was rich. And Dushyant was relieved that his alias had been successful. His lie was safe. Or at least that was what he thought. For Priya, this was the biggest catch she had had: a genuine millionaire, someone who wanted true love and not just a clandestine romp and a one-night stand.

Dushyant could have just easily gone into the 'battle zone', shot off a few shots and retreated to his normal life. Why did he choose to remain in the battle zone, pretending to look for true love? Maybe he was trying to prolong the feel-good, endorphin-laced moments that he felt outside of his vacuous life.

The one element Priya had refined in her modus operandi, post her being arrested on the cheating case was she no longer responded to men who were from the city or the state. On Tinder, she only targeted men who were from outside Rajasthan, and who were only probably passing through. She did not want any more hassle with residents.

And so the game went on! But there was a twist for Priya.

On 7 March 2018, Gurujar's complaint of January 2018, which had sparked off an investigation on Priya and her blackmailing tactics, concluded. Investigation Officer (IO) Nidhi arrested her. They say, the biggest of criminals panic on seeing a cop in uniform. And that is what happened with Priya. As soon as she was arrested, she confessed to her crime of threatening and blackmailing Gurujar. The police recovered Rs 4,14,000 from her.

Bhopal Singh, the SHO of Vaishali Nagar, became aware that the girl standing in front of him was actually a seasoned criminal. 'Seth has a criminal past which include ATM loot bid. She had also been in the past involved in escort services.'[32]

In an interview given to Deepika Narayan Bharadwaj, IO Nidhi Dhaka speaks about how difficult it was to convince the law that a girl was at fault. She faced numerous challenges to get police custody of Priya and had to furnish multiple evidence in front of the judge despite Priya's past criminal records![33]

Inspector Nidhi Dhaka went on to explain, 'It is not easy to convince someone that the girl is at fault. Everyone believes a girl if she says she has been raped. We don't face any problem in issuing a *challan* in that case and arrest the man. But if a man complains that a woman is blackmailing him, then it's very difficult as it is against the norm. When I went to the court to get her police custody in this case and take her on remand, it took me quite some time to convince the judge and tell him that I have arrested this woman on basis of all these evidence. The judge saw the file thoroughly, and only then allowed a police custody.'[34]

When asked by Bharadwaj, if the IO thinks that women are misusing the anti-rape laws, the IO immediately said: 'Absolutely! It is being misused in a lot of cases. If you see in this case itself, she first has sexual relationship with consent and then threatens to file a rape case. Because this is what she does; develop relationship by her own will but then threaten and demand money later.'

While in custody at the Vaishali Nagar Police Station, Priya continued to be arrogance personified with not an iota of remorse. She demanded she be allowed to smoke and was always trying to seek attention.

Priya spent five days in remand and then was granted bail on 12 March 2018.

Priya was free to hunt again.

As soon as she was free, Priya tried to mend her image and appear innocent and goody-two shoes to the outside world. The *Hindustan Times* had interviewed Priya on 21 March in connection with the extortion charge by Gurujar Singh. Priya continued to deny the extortion charge and the fake pregnancy. 'I loved him, but he left me in the lurch. He even beat me when we lived in Noida,' she said.[35]

But for now, she was back to being with Dushyant.

Priya must have read the story about the donkey and the carrot as a child, because that is exactly what she did with Dushyant. She did not allow Dushyant to have sex with her. She always kept it out of his reach, ensuring the 'millionaire' boyfriend returned. With Gurujar gone, she needed a new sugar daddy or someone who would fund her expensive lifestyle.

On the hunt for new targets, she came upon a profile of a man named Dikshant Kamra. She liked his looks. She swiped right.

When I spoke with Gur Bhoopendra Singh and asked him if Priya had the intention of conning Kamra as well, the IO replied saying Priya had confessed that she had liked him and she was in love with him.

But that still did not answer my question: at the time of her swiping right, what was her true intention? Was Kamra going to be conned like the rest of them or she had found him good looking and had been attracted to him? The answer lies with Priya. And I fear, we will never know the truth, as they are now accomplices in a heinous crime. And she would like him to be behind bars just like her.

But after having studied criminals over the past fourteen years, my guess is Dikshant was supposed to be another victim of hers. He just turned out to be prince charming. Unknown to him, his fate was oscillating between the devil (being conned) and the deep blue sea (helping her to murder Dushyant).

'I met Priya through the Tinder app. We spoke and met the next day,' Dikshant recalled, 'we started speaking on the phone and got emotionally attached.'[36]

Interestingly, in the beginning, Priya treated Dikshant as a target. Like a juggler, she added one more spinning ball to her hand. She constructed a new story for Dikshant. She told him that she worked with Vasu Holidays, a travel agency. Dikshant fell for the story. Seeing her lavish lifestyle of stylish clothes, expensive watches and perfumes, branded bags and shoes, and Marlboro Lights at her fingertips, Dikshant was convinced Priya had a legit job.

Unknowingly Dikshant's fate was balancing at the edge of a knife. It could have gone the other way. But he was good looking. According to a police official who was part of the investigating team, 'Seth had met Kamra through Tinder early in April or February and both had taken a strong liking to each other. Within a span of a few days, they decided to live together and took a flat on rent in Bajaj Nagar . . . Seth realized that Kamra was smart and fearless, unlike her previous boyfriends and they got serious about each other,' the official said.[37]

When I asked the Jhotwara SHO Gur Bhoopendra Singh why Priya spared Dikshant and did not cheat him, he said, '*Unke soch-vichaar mein bonding ho gayi.* They were similar in their thoughts.'

Dikshant was living with Lakshya, and it was time for karma to bring the three together.

Dikshant introduced the two of them to each other. Soon, the three of them were hanging out together. For Lakshya, Priya's lavish lifestyle of alcohol and drugs was something straight out of the movies. And this also meant that Priya became the source of the good things for the unemployed boys.

There was an age gap between Priya (twenty-seven) and Dikshant (twenty-one) which made the latter impressionable and he was easily emotionally malleable. Within a few days, Dikshant and Priya became close and Dikshant poured his heart out to Priya regarding his background, and his failed stint in Mumbai and how he owed people lakhs of rupees. And this is what probably saved Dikshant from meeting the fate of a Dushyant or being conned like the others. Hearing about his debt, Priya probably realized that she would not be able to squeeze him for more money. And by this time, she had also fallen for his looks and his swag.

They both yearned for the good life, aspired for the expensive things and both of them were struggling with money (except Dikshant didn't know that of Priya, at that time). Although Priya was conning people every day, she was also spending the money on an unreasonably extravagant lifestyle. She was earning with one hand, and spending with two fists. When love beckoned, Priya and Dikshant decided to move in together in March 2018. Priya, the master storyteller that she was, constructed another story. This one, for the owner of the flat.

Mrs Neelam Yadav owned Flat no 402, Eden Garden, Anita Colony, Bajaj Nagar. Like every flat owner, she too was apprehensive of leasing out her place to single men or women. 'This generation cannot be trusted' was the universal opinion of all flat owners. And so when Priya approached Mrs Yadav via the real-estate broker Rajkumar, the flat owner wanted to know every little detail before she leased out her flat.

Priya said that she was from a wealthy family and was a YouTube documentary film-maker. Furthermore, she introduced herself and Dikshant as a young, much in love, newly married couple. The trick worked, and the monthly rent was fixed at Rs 27,000.

Ironically, it would be a documentary film maker who would make Priya famous and expose her Machiavellian character to the world. But we are jumping way ahead . . .

Once the 'couple' moved in, their life revolved around snorting cocaine, smoking up marijuana and drinking copious amounts of alcohol. According to the police, Priya squandered all the money she earned by duping people, on this hedonistic lifestyle, which was way beyond her means.

According to some reports, when Dikshant moved in with Priya, he had no clue about her duplicity and 'contrepreneur' avatar. He assumed the story she had shared about her life with him to be the truth. She was a 'normal' person with a 'normal' job. But after moving in with Priya, the truth slowly started unravelling before his eyes.

Priya did not have a legit job. Vasu Holidays was a figment of her imagination. And more frighteningly, she was a con woman.

At this point, as a reader, you must be wondering: why didn't Dikshant escape? He was smart enough to understand what Priya was doing was a crime.

'Later I got to know about her reality, but I couldn't find a way to leave her and escape,' is how he explained it after his arrest.[38]

What Priya offered Dikshant, who was struggling to make ends meet, was a good life that included great food, designer clothes and copious amounts of alcohol. So, instead of scampering away in fear, Dikshant chose to embrace this readily available lifestyle, where he didn't have to worry about the next pay cheque.

One of the indications of Priya having truly fallen in love with Dikshant was she getting his name tattooed on her arm.

Dikshant, on the other hand, went one step ahead. Instead of getting a tattoo, he, like a good boy, told his mother about Priya.

Meanwhile, Priya's younger sister visited their flat at Eden Garden and met Dikshant. Priya confided in her that she wanted to get married. Priya's sister did not approve.

Priya was headstrong and always did things her way. So she decided to ignore her sister's disapproval. Priya had left the structure of the family years ago when she stepped out of Falna. And she was answerable to no one but herself.

Meanwhile, Dikshant's constant whining about his debt and the threat of his creditors turning up stressed out Priya. He was worried sick about what the creditors would do to him, if they located him. While Priya kept reassuring him that she would find a way to solve the issue, while stepping out to continue her 'social work' of conning married men.

In a day she would meet at least three to four such targets.[39] And income from this 'social work' paid for the rent, her lifestyle and, of course, Dikshant and Lakshya's alcohol.

Priya wanted to end her boyfriend's troubles, so when Priya told Dikshant that she had found the perfect candidate who they would kidnap, they all felt a sense of hope and relief.

As per the charge sheet, Priya told Dikshant that she knew someone named Bivan (sic) Kohli who is from Delhi, and is rich. They could kidnap him and ask for ransom and get Rs 20-25 lakh easily. Priya Seth told Dikshant that Bivan Kohli believes her so much that he will come wherever she calls him.

The question was: how would she lure him to their house? Priya assured Dikshant that Vivan was in love with her, and he would do anything she told him to do. She would lure him home with the promise of a 'good' evening.

After this discussion, Priya and Dikshant chalked out a plan to kidnap Bivan Kohli and ask for ransom.

It was time for Stage One of the game . . .

Chapter Seven

The Kidnapping

2 May 2018, Wednesday.

What Priya had been holding off for the past two months as bait was now offered to Dushyant, aka Vivan Kohli, on a platter. The date for consummating their relationship was set as 2 May 2018.

Dushyant was overjoyed. He was finally going to 'score'. Dushyant planned for the day, which included the alibi he would give his family if they questioned him. Priya had told him that she would call him up and tell him where to meet her and then they would go to her house.

At this time all Dikshant and Lakshya knew was that Priya had identified a target from whom she would extort the money to pay the lakhs that Dikshant owed, and also to fund their life for the next few months. Lakshya, who was Dikshant's childhood friend, became privy to the real Priya and her real occupation, once Dikshant was made aware. Lakshya too stayed back and did not run away. He too wanted to enjoy the good life that Priya's dubious earnings offered.

When Priya revealed that she was going to be bringing Vivan home that day, there was an air of nervousness tinged with excitement at Eden Garden. Dikshant was suddenly alert as it dawned on him that he was staring at the point of no return!

When Priya had first shared the plan of kidnapping somebody for ransom, Dikshant had baulked for an instant, according to the police. But he too saw the 'merit' in this shortcut to acquire money in an instant. He wanted to erase his debts as soon as possible.

At 5 p.m., Priya asked Dikshant to call Lakshya to their Eden Garden flat. At this point, Lakshya had no clue what was about to unfold that evening. Priya primed them with drinks and ganja. Soon, they were high and happy.

At approximately 6 p.m., Priya messaged Dushyant, setting in motion the dastardly plan. She told him that she would meet him below Bhaskar Pulia, Tonk Road at around 7.30 p.m.

Dushyant was back from work and relaxing when the call came in. He sprang up for a shower and started getting dressed. His wife, Bittu, found this rather unusual because once her husband returned home from work, he usually didn't go out again.

'Kahan ja rahe ho?' (Where are you going?) Bittu asked him.

Dushyant avoided looking his wife in the eye and hurriedly said, 'Urgent kaam hai' (There is urgent work) as he slipped into his Nike sneakers.

'Nikki beta, what work do you have in the night? You have just come back home!'

Rameshwar joined in the conversation. Dushyant's pet name was Nikki. Even his father thought that this was unusual behaviour.

Dushyant realized he had to make a credible excuse to get his family off his back. And so he did. 'One of the company vehicles carrying sand from the river has been seized by the police.[40] You know how the police keep targeting mining companies . . .'

That seemed to do the trick. And for good measure, he added, 'I will be back in an hour.'

'Papa, I am taking your car.' With that, at 7 p.m. on 2 May 2018, Dushyant walked out of his Shivpuri Extension home in Jaipur for the final time. He got into his father's Hyundai i10 and drove off.

Priya knew their lives were about to change forever. She had already manifested the riches and money that the scam would bring them. She was very proud of the way she had handled Vivan so far, the way she had seduced him, kept him dangling and convinced him she wasn't after his money. This was going to be her lottery ticket—the biggest payload.

She called him up to ensure he was on his way. Dushyant was excited. On his way, he stopped at a medical store and bought a packet of condoms.[41] He then stopped at a liquor store and bought a bottle of red wine. He wanted the night to be as romantic as possible. Priya called him up again.

'Yes, yes, I am on my way.' Hearing this, Priya left her flat at approximately 7 p.m. for the rendezvous.

While Priya was gone, Dikshant narrated the plan to Lakshya. Lakshya was immediately nervous and did not want to get involved, 'We will let him go, right? After we get the money?' Priya had hatched a new story for Lakshya. She had tutored Dikshant to tell Lakshya that this 'target' was a man who was harassing and troubling her, and therefore they would extract money from him as punishment. Dikshant assured him it was going to be a simple operation. 'We will keep him hostage and demand a ransom. Once we receive the money, we will let him go . . .'

Lakshya relaxed a bit.

Meanwhile, at approximately 7.45 p.m., Priya called up Vivan aka Dushyant, giving him directions as to where she was waiting. When Dushyant picked her up, both were excited to see each other. Dushyant was excited in anticipation of the passionate night that lay ahead, while Priya was excited about the money she would have within the next few hours!

Priya sat in the car and smiled at Dushyant, who seemed unable to hide his excitement.

'Head towards Bajaj Nagar,' Priya gave directions to her flat.

Mary Howitt was an English poet whose poem 'The Spider and the Fly', published in 1829, became one of the most well-known poems because of its opening line: 'Will you walk into my parlour?' The poem tells of a cunning spider that entraps a fly in its web through the use of seduction and manipulation. It is a cautionary tale against people who use flattery, seduction and charm to disguise their true intentions. Priya was the cunning spider, while Dushyant was the naive fly.

'Will you walk into my parlour?' said a spider to a fly;
' 'Tis the prettiest little parlour that ever you did spy'

'You can park the car inside the building compound,' Priya instructed him when they reached Eden Garden at around 8 p.m.

The way into my parlour is up a winding stair,
And I have many pretty things to shew when you are there.'

'Which floor are you on?' Dushyant asked as Priya led him towards the lift.

'It's 402. Fourth floor,' she replied getting into the lift.

I'm sure you must be weary, with soaring up so high,

Will you rest upon my little bed?' said the spider to the fly.

There are pretty curtains drawn around, the sheets are fine and thin;

And if you like to rest awhile, I'll snugly tuck you in.'

'I am so glad that we are finally getting to spend time together,' Priya said as she held his hand in his.

Priya opened the door to her flat and they went in.

'Nice place!' Dushyant remarked as he kept the bottle down.

'I will just freshen up,' said Priya as she exited the sitting room.

Dushyant looked around as he made himself comfortable on the sofa. The flat was bereft of any fancy furniture. In fact, it looked rather ordinary. Then suddenly, out of nowhere, two men appeared on the scene and pounced on him. Dushyant was shell-shocked, not knowing how to react. The men started beating him up. Dushyant thought that they were intruders in the flat. He screamed, 'Call the police. There are intruders!'

One of them hit Dushyant on his face and his head started to reel. He fought back as much as he could. One of them was much bigger than him. He pinned Dushyant against the sofa. Dushyant yelled for Priya to come and help. Priya ran into the room. Dushyant screamed, 'Help me! Call the police!' There was a beat, and then suddenly Priya too leapt on Dushyant and started beating him up.

Dushyant could not comprehend what was happening. How could his girlfriend be siding with these intruders? What was going on? And why was she hitting him? All his dreams of spending a romantic and intimate evening with Priya came crashing down as he realized the three of them were indeed a team!

Chapter Eight

The Twist

2 May 2018, Wednesday.

The trio sat down and caught their breath. They were sweating. For the love of God, Dushyant could not decipher what was going on. He found himself tied up to a chair, his face and body ached from the merciless blows that had pummelled him.

Was Priya married? Was this her husband and his friend who had caught her cheating? If so, why was Priya joining them and beating him up? Everything was a blur.

Dikshant came closer to the chair on which Dushyant was tied up. Dushyant flinched, anticipating another rain of blows. Priya took out Dushyant's wallet from the back pocket of his trousers. When she took out his ATM card, she was taken aback.

On the ATM card was the name Dushyant Sharma. She took out the Driver's License (RJ14/DLC/11/52XXXX) too and then his Pan Card (HCBPS3XXXX) to make sure she had got the name right. It was indeed Dushyant Sharma.

She could taste the rising bile at the back of her throat as panic and anxiety started taking over her body.

Priya carefully went through each and every card in his wallet hoping at least one of them will say Vivan Kohli.

There was a Union Bank debit card with the number 60XXX27553XXXXX printed on it.

A health insurance medical card on which 'health privilege' was printed.

A Karnataka Bank debit card bearing number 60XXXXXXXX34663.

A Rajasthan Technical Enrolment card bearing Enrolment no. 9EXXXXX40P012.

And his Aadhaar card with number XXXX9794XXXX.

All of them said 'Dushyant Sharma'.

'What is your name? Are you not Vivan Kohli?' Priya screamed as she grabbed Dushyant's face menacingly in her hand.

Tera asli naam kya hai? Tu hai kaun? Yeh Dushyant kaun hai?' (What is your real name? Who are you? Who is this Dushyant?) Priya's coy 'girlfriend' image that she had maintained with Vivan over the past two months dissipated as her true, foul-mouthed avatar emerged. She slapped him across the face and screamed for him to answer.

Through tears, Dushyant spilled the beans. 'I am Dushyant Sharma. I am not Vivan Kohli. Vivan was just a name I used for Tinder.'

Priya was on tenterhooks, hoping that would be the extent of the lie and the mix-up. She was still hoping the name was fake but that at least his riches were real.

Dikshant could not believe what he just heard and snatched the wallet from Priya and took out the

Aadhaar Card. The card number A7800979XXXXX had the name Dushyant Sharma on it.

'But you are a crorepati, right? You are rich?' Priya asked, desperation obvious in her voice. The entire thing finally dawned on Dushyant. He put two and two together and arrived at 22! The three of them were working together and he had been kidnapped! His 'girlfriend' had laid a perfect trap. The realization hit him hard as tears streamed down his cheeks.

'No, I am not rich. I don't have a business. I am just an ordinary guy working in a mining company. I am not a millionaire!' Dushyant blurted out.

'Where are you from?' Priya screamed, holding him by the collar of his shirt.

'I am from here. I am . . . I am from Jaipur,' Dushyant whimpered.

Priya's new modus operandi had mostly been to trap outsiders, or middle-aged men, both of whom would not dare report her to the police. But this was not just a twist in the tale but the mother-of-all-fuckups! He was not only broke but also a local.

All hell broke loose.

'*Madarchod!!*' (Motherfucker!) Dikshant screamed and lunged at Dushyant. He rained blows on him. Dushyant's nose was bleeding and his lip had received a cut from the blows.

'Please let me go! Please! I have nothing to give you,' Dushyant pleaded.

Priya sat with her head in her hands as she realized that her perfectly laid-out plan had fallen flat. And then, like a true criminal, she switched to Plan B and took charge the situation.

'*Iska mobile nikaal* (Extract his mobile phone). Give it to me!' Priya instructed Lakshya, who then took out Dushyant's mobile and handed it to her. She then took out all the credit and debit cards from his wallet.

'*Chal, Dushyant Sharma, ab bata tera ATM passwords bata*' (Come on, Dushyant Sharma, tell us your ATM passwords). Priya demanded.

For a middle-class person, an ATM password is akin to the key to Fort Knox or the RBI. It is a well-guarded secret that cannot be shared at any cost. It's one's life savings gathered over the years through sweat and toil. How could one just hand over the keys? And so Dushyant kept mum.

'*Nahi bolega?*' (You won't reveal it?) Dikshant hit him again, drawing fresh blood.

The three of them kept beating him up till Dushyant finally gave in.

Dikshant, Priya and Lakshya went into a huddle. The realization that Dushyant was a middle-class bloke had hit them hard and they discussed the next step: what is a realistic amount they could demand of him? An amount that he or is family is able to cough up?

'*Ab sunn! Zinda rehna hai toh dus lakh ka arrangement kar*' (Listen, if you want to stay alive, arrange for Rs 10 lakh), Priya demanded.

'If you don't pay the money, you won't get out of here alive!' Dikshant threatened.

'From where will my family or I get that kind of money? We are middle-class people. Please let me go . . .' Dushyant wailed.

* * *

Flashback to 2012.

Meenakshi Thapa, or as some newspapers have called her, Meenakshi Thapar, was born in Dehradun with dreams of becoming an actress. And so she headed to Mumbai. She struggled like many of the star-struck dreamers who arrive in the city of dreams. But she managed to get a small role in a movie in 2011. It was called *404: Error Not Found*. This was followed by another small role in *Pakauu* (2012) and then came her big break in the big-banner, big-budget *Heroine* (2012), which starred Kareena Kapoor Khan in the titular role.

Meenakshi often boasted about her family's wealth and how she was related to the royal family of Nepal. One of her co-stars was a bit actor, fellow-struggler Amit Jaiswal. Hearing this, he hatched a plan with his girlfriend Preeti Surin. They lured Meenakshi on a trip to Gorakhpur, Uttar Pradesh, to meet a producer. There, they kept her hostage and demanded Rs 15 lakh from her family. That is when the truth unfolded.[42]

In reality, neither Meenakshi nor her family was rich. Her mother somehow managed to pay Rs 60,000. The duo killed Meenakshi, decapitated her and threw her head out of a moving bus, and her body in a septic tank. They were eventually caught.

This sensational case was featured in 2012 across two episodes in the true-crime television show that I created, wrote and produced called *Savdhaan India*. In every episode, a seekh/lesson was attached to the crime story which would alert the viewers to look out for criminals and criminal behaviour and keep them safe from harm.

Unfortunately, Dushyant had not seen the episodes, nor had he read the newspapers, or else he would have taken some lessons from Meenakshi's errors.

* * *

The biggest mistake that Dushyant made was to lie. The second mistake was to be guided by his misguided libido. What began as an online affair, limited to the virtual space, spilled over into the real world, luring Dushyant into the spider web of the experienced and devious Priya.

But now, Priya, Dikshant and Lakshya had some thinking to do as their initial plan had backfired. Never in her wildest dreams had Priya imagined that a bluff master like herself would be fooled and outwitted once again! Her rage built up inside her. Now, they were battling with what to do next.

Chapter Nine

What Next?

2 May 2018, Wednesday.

'I can give you Rs 8 lakh right away. But you have to promise to let me go,' Dushyant had a brainwave. When you are facing death, the body goes into fight or flight mode.

The trio looked at Dushyant incredulously. *Was Dushyant on drugs? Was he hallucinating? Had he lost his mind?* They wondered.

'He is bluffing,' Lakshya piped up.

'From where will you get the money? Out of thin air?' Priya spat her words on his face.

'No. I have it in my wallet. There is a cheque.'

Dikshant scavenged through the wallet and pulled out the cheque. It was a 'Self' cheque signed by Mahesh Yadav for the amount of Rs 8 lakh. Priya could suddenly feel a change in her fortunes. She hadn't anticipated that the ransom money would turn up so quickly and effortlessly, and from right under their noses. She broke out into an excited smile as she held the cheque in her hands.

'Whose cheque is this?' Priya's aggression was replaced by excitement.

'Mahesh orders river sand for his construction work through me and I place an order for it with my company. He had handed me this 'Self' cheque for a past order. He was supposed to put money in his account and then I was supposed to deposit this. You can deposit it and take all the money,' Dushyant pleaded. It was approximately 11. 30 p.m.

'Chal, phone laga iss ko aur poochh ussne account mein paisa dala hai ki nahi?' (Come on, call him and ask him if he has deposited money in the account or not.) Priya ordered.

Dushyant called Mahesh Yadav. He prayed and hoped that Mahesh would have deposited the money, making this cheque valid. This was going to be his way out of this mess.

'Hello, Mahesh?' Dushyant's voice was wavering. One of the trio hissed, 'Put the phone on speaker mode,' Dushyant switched on the speaker.

'Hi Dushyant. You are calling so late in the night. Everything okay?'

'Listen, do you remember the "self" cheque you had given me the other day for Rs 8 lakh?' Dushyant held his breath.

'Yes of course I remember. I had told you to hold on and not deposit it till I had funds,' Mahesh replied. Dushyant breathed easy.

'I need the money desperately. Can I deposit the cheque now? I need urgent funds. Have you deposited the amount?' Dushyant knew this was the moment that would either help his escape or spell his doom.

There was silence on the other side, and then Mahesh's voice was heard again.

'What to tell you? I have had a solid cash crunch. I have had no funds to deposit in my account. So please don't deposit the cheque yet,' Mahesh said. The world came crashing down on Dushyant.

Chandramohan 'Charlie' Sharma, played by Shah Rukh Khan in the film *Happy New Year* (2014), mouthed the epic dialogue, *'Kismat badi kutti cheez hai, saali kabhi bhi palat jaati hai.'* (Destiny is a bitch, it can flip on you anytime.)

Mahesh had no clue about the situation at the other end of the line and that he probably could have saved Dushyant's life if he had told Dushyant to deposit the cheque at that moment.

But *'kutti kismat'* had ensured Mahesh had had a run of bad luck and was unable to spruce up his bank account with fresh funds.

And this is truly what fascinates me: that everything in life is connected. If Mahesh had tried harder to recoup his funds, then he probably would have been able to deposit it and thus saved Dushyant's life. But how was he to know what was going to happen?

Dushyant realized he was screwed. He was about to scream and curse Mahesh when Dikshant suddenly disconnected the phone. Priya, who had, just a few minutes ago started seeing the light at the end of the tunnel, now realized the tunnel had caved in on her.

They all pummelled him with blows and kicks.

Meanwhile, back at Shivpuri Extension, Rameshwar looked at his watch. It had been over two hours since Dushyant had left home saying he would be back in an hour. It was around 9.15 p.m. when he tried his son's number.

Dushyant's phone started ringing. The trio stared at the phone. Dushyant tried to lunge for it using his body, as his hands were tied. Dikshant kicked him away from the phone and grabbed it.

'Who is it?' Priya asked.

'His dad,' Dikshant replied.

'Disconnect it!' Priya commanded.

Dikshant obeyed.

The trio did not know which way to move. What at first had seemed an easy grab-and-go plan was now lying completely disheveled.

'What did he say?' Bittu inquired of her father-in-law, whose brows were creased with worry.

'*Usne call disconnect kar diya.*' (He disconnected the call.)

'Why would he do that?' Bittu was almost speaking to herself now, questioning this strange behaviour of her husband's.

'Maybe he is still busy with work,' Rameshwar conjectured.

'You don't call him now. I will call him after half an hour and speak with him. You and Mother go have dinner.'

At 9.45 p.m., Bittu called up her husband.

The phone kept ringing. Dushyant kept staring at his phone. A hundred regrets went through his head at that moment seeing his wife's name pop up on the mobile screen. *If only . . .*

Why did he create the fake account on Tinder? Why did he look for sex outside of marriage? Why did he have to match with Priya, who turned out to be an evil woman? He realized the situation he currently found himself in, was his own doing. Dushyant started crying.

'If we don't let him speak with his family, they will think something is amiss and they might even go to the police,'

Dikshant's mind was functioning like that of a seasoned criminal. 'Let him speak to his family so he can assure them he is fine and then we will switch off the phone,' Dikshant continued.

Priya turned to Dushyant and threatened him.

'What is the point of crying now? Listen, speak to your wife and make up an excuse. Tell her you will be back by morning. That you are caught up in some urgent work. And remember, no tricks!'

Dikshant accepted the call and put the phone on speaker and placed it near Dushyant's face. Dushyant's eyes darted towards his captors. He had the strong urge to scream 'help', but he knew Bittu would not be able to do anything from afar, and that it might also put his own life in danger.

'Hello? Where are you? Why did you disconnect Baba's call? Why aren't you home yet?' Bittu, who had been waiting for nearly three hours, shot off a salvo of questions.

'Bittu . . .' Dushyant's voice faltered.

Dikshant threatened to hit him.

'Are you okay?' Bittu asked.

Dushyant controlled his emotions, 'Yes, I am okay. Actually, the police have confiscated six to seven trucks of gravel belonging to the company. And they are demanding a fine of around Rs 10 lakh.'

Priya mumbled, asking him to hang up the phone.

'I am going to return late night or in the morning. Don't worry. Go to bed,' Dushyant assured Bittu.

Before he could say anything more, Dikshant disconnected the phone.

Bittu could sense that something was wrong, but she trusted what her husband had said. She would later recall hearing the voice of a woman speaking behind her husband. Dushyant had mentioned to her earlier that the police had increased their surveillance and searching of the mining companies for illegal sand mining. Bittu had no clue that her husband had been beaten black and blue, was being held captive and tied up, and was at the mercy of three cold-blooded kidnappers.

'People will be saying all sorts of things about him, but they don't know him. I know him,' Bittu told a journalist.[43] Even after Dushyant was murdered, Bittu continued to be in shock and denial. After all, it was unfathomable for her that Dushyant, of all people, was leading this Dr Jekyll and Mr Hyde kind of existence.

An hour later when the family tried to call again, they found Dushyant's phone switched off. They went into panic mode. This was very unusual. Their obedient son had always informed them about his whereabouts and was accessible on the phone. This was a huge anomaly. They kept trying his phone through the night, but to no avail.

With tears of worry streaming down her face, Vaijanti started praying, while Rameshwar now started making phone calls to relatives. Seeing the lights of the house on at this time of night, their neighbours and well-wishers trooped in.

'What happened, Rameshwarji?' a neighbour asked, concerned.

'Arre dekhiye na! Itni raat ho gayi aur Dushyant abhi tak ghar nahi aaya.' (Dushyant has not returned home, even at this hour of the night.) Rameshwar was worried.

'But he is always home by six in the evening . . .'

Nishant Sharma, Dushyant's cousin had just celebrated his daughter's birthday and returned home after the party, at around 10 p.m., when he learnt about Dushyant. His younger brother Vishwas and his mother both went to look for Dushyant on a motorcycle but to no avail.

When past midnight there was no sign of Dushyant, the relatives who had turned up at the house as well as the neighbours took to the streets to search for Dushyant. They alerted every police station in the vicinity hoping they might throw up some clues, but the search came to naught.

'Let Nikki come back in the morning, I am going to scold him and tell him not to do this again. How can he be away this late in the night?' Rameshwar said, his brows creased with worry.

Meanwhile, back at Eden Garden, Dushyant was going through hell. Lakshya and Dikshant had tied his hands and feet with a black cable wire. They gagged his mouth with a piece of cloth. Dushyant's eyes widened in horror, and he shook his head from side to side trying to avoid what was happening. They put a polythene bag over his face and threw him on the bed.

As Dushyant tried to breathe, the polythene bag expanded and deflated. He felt a searing pain on his left cheekbone as a punch landed on his face. And then he gasped and struggled to breathe as a kick in his stomach knocked the wind out of him. With his hands and feet tied, and his face covered, he had no way to fight back or to even anticipate and fend off the blows. He was literally in the dark. The trio kept hitting him. They laughed as they seemed to be enjoying themselves.

Dushyant lay curled up in a fetal position on the bed, crying. Every time they had to ask him anything, they took off the polythene bag from Dushyant's face. Dushyant squinted as the light hit his eyes and seeing his attackers in front of him, he started grunting desperately, fearing their attack. Dikshant ripped off the cloth gag from Dushyant's mouth. Immediately, Dushyant inhaled a lungful of air and then coughed as his parched throat irritated him. And this went on.

'What do we do about dinner?' Lakshya asked. They did not want to order from the online apps as that would mean a delivery boy turning up at their doorstep, and the possibility of him discovering their crime. So one of them headed out to buy dinner like it was just another normal day.

Chapter Ten

The Ransom Call

3 May 2018, Thursday.

Dushyant woke up with acute pain all over his body. He had been beaten up so much that he could barely move. He groaned in pain. From where he lay on the bed, he could see his abductors.

The trio had barely slept through the night. They were at their wits' end planning how to monetize the situation and get away with it. Their main concern was that Dushyant was a local and if he was set free after receiving the ransom amount, it was highly likely that Dushyant would go to the police.

'But how do we get the ransom transferred to us? They will track our accounts,' Priya was on the ball and correct in her assumptions.

Dikshant had a plan. 'First, we will get the ransom money in Dushyant's account. From there, we will withdraw some money using his ATM card. The rest of the money, Dushyant will transfer it to another account belonging to someone

I know. From there, we will withdraw the cash or through a 'self'-addressed cheque. This way, the police will not be able to trace the ransom money to us.'

* * *

Meanwhile, Dushyant's residence was covered in a pall of worry and gloom. Nobody knew where he was, and calls made to his colleagues and friends all resulted in zero leads. His mother was red eyed from weeping, and dark circles had formed under her eyes for not having slept through the night. His father sat stone-faced and helpless, not knowing what to do next. Bittu was busy dividing her time between stressing and taking care of their kid. What was worrisome was that her husband's phone was switched off.

When his wife started crying, Rameshwar tried to reassure her, 'He is protected, don't worry. All the amulets and the rings that he is wearing will protect him from any harm.'

Neighbours as always contributed meaningless and irritable inputs.

'Maybe his phone has been stolen.'

'Maybe he fell asleep at the office.'

'The phone battery must have died.'

* * *

Priya and Dikshant made Dushyant sit up.

'This is the plan,' Priya began, 'You want to go back home, right?'

Dushyant nodded his head, not knowing what to expect next.

'So, you are going to call up your father and ask him for the money. You are going to tell him to send Rs 10 lakh to your bank account, or else we will kill you,' Priya's bloodshot eyes were wide and scary.

'From where will my father get the money?' Dushyant knew that his father did not have this kind of money.

'Do you think we care? Just speak to your father and convince him to send us the money,' Dikshant held him by the collar of his shirt.

Dikshant scrolled through the phone and stopped at 'Papa' and dialled the number.

* * *

It was approximately 9.45 a.m. when Dushyant's name flashed on Rameshwar's mobile screen. There was pandemonium, excitement, panic all rolled into one.

'*Nikki ka phone hain.*' (Nikki is calling.) Rameshwar yelled to his wife, who came running, along with Bittu.

Rameshwar accepted the call and put the phone to his ear, 'Hello, Nikki beta . . .'

Dushyant started crying immediately, 'Papa, they will kill me. Please give them Rs 10 lakh *aur mujhe bacha lo.* Please save me.'

The world slipped from under Rameshwar's feet, 'Nikki? Are you okay? Who are these people, Beta?'

'Please, please save me . . . *Mujhe bacha lo,*' Dushyant pleaded.

Nishant, who was present during this call, would later recall in court that he could hear the distinct voices of two men in the background as they kept beating Dushyant. This was followed by the voice of a woman who said, 'I will kill you if you don't disconnect the phone.'

Before Rameshwar could ask anything more, a female voice came on the phone as Priya took charge and grabbed the phone from Dushyant. *'Agar tere bete ko bachana hai na, toh tere bete ke khatay mein dus lakh rupaye jama karaday.'* (If you want to save your son, then transfer Rs 10 lakh to his bank account.)

'Mere paas abhi dus lakh nahi hain, mujhe time de do chaar baje tak . . .' (I don't have Rs 10 lakh with me right now, give me time till 4 p.m. to arrange for it.) Rameshwar requested.

Priya was a sharp cookie: what we would have missed, she caught on. We would have perhaps replied saying, 'So by when will you be able to deposit the money?' But Priya caught on to the first half of Rameshwar's reply, 'I don't have Rs 10 lakh with me right now.' This clearly meant that Rameshwar had some amount with him at that moment and she shot back.

'Toh abhi kitna jama kara dega?' (So how much will you be able to transfer now?) Priya barked.

'Mere paas abhi do-teen lakh hoga. Mein ek ghante mein jama kar doonga.' (I have about Rs 2–3 lakh now. I can deposit it in an hour.) Rameshwar was already thinking about the fixed deposit he had.

'Teen lakh, bees minute mein jama kara. Nahi toh maar dungi.' (Deposit Rs 3 lakh within twenty minutes or else we will kill your son.)

'Mere Nikki ko kuchh mat karna. Main saath lakh shaam tak intezaam kar lunga.' (Please don't harm my Nikki. I will arrange Rs 7 lakh by the evening.)

Rameshwar begged.

At this point, Priya started using filthy, abusive language to reprimand and threaten Rameshwar, and then disconnected the phone.

At a later interview, Rameshwar would recall, 'I begged her for mercy, but she started swearing in the worst manner. I have never heard a woman swear like that in my life.'[44]

Priya was good at her game of hoodwinking, honey trapping and conning, but she was a lousy negotiator and kidnapper. Perhaps influenced by watching too many Hollywood movies, she expected the father to open a mysterious laptop and do a wire transfer from the Cayman Islands account. She was indeed expecting the transfer to happen in twenty minutes!

Back at Dushyant's house, his mother broke down and wailed. The neighbours rushed in. Bittu could not believe what was going on. Why would someone kidnap her husband? They were not rich, nor were they famous. Nothing was making sense to anybody. But Rameshwar was clear about what needed to be done. He had to get his son freed at any cost. And he knew he had very little time.

He quickly put on a shirt. Then he went to the old cupboard, took out his bank papers and rushed out. The clock was ticking. The world seemed to darken in front of Vaijanti's eyes. Her knees buckled and she lost consciousness.

The greatest tragedy for any parent is to lose their child and Rameshwar had experienced that pain twice in his life. He could not bear the thought of having to carry the bier again—this time of his only surviving son. It was approximately 10 a.m. when Rameshwar rushed out of the house and to the bank, with tears streaming down his face.

Back at Eden, nothing was idyllic. Priya was hyperventilating and overexcited. In a matter of a few hours, the prey had become a liability.

Dikshant took her aside and asked, 'When you were speaking to his father, you kept saying you will kill him, you weren't serious, right?'

There was panic in Lakshya's face as well, 'That wasn't the plan. Priya. You said we will kidnap him, threaten him, take the ransom and then let him go!'

Priya's nostrils flared and her face screwed up in anger and disgust. She looked like an angry reptile who had missed her prey. She spoke loudly. 'I had thought this guy was Vivan Kohli and that he was rich. And the fact that he was from out of town. It was going to be easy money! But this swine has turned out to be middle class and a local and therefore he can register a complaint!'

Hearing this, Dushyant immediately spoke up, trying his best to convince his captors, 'You keep the money. I will not complain to the police. I will not do anything of the like. I will not take any action against you. It's a promise.'

'Maybe your father will not transfer the money at all. Maybe he is just buying time,' Priya hissed. 'Maybe your father has gone to the police to lodge a complaint.'

At the mention of the police, Lakshya's knees buckled and the reality of the situation they were in started to finally sink in for Dikshant.

Priya was on tenterhooks. 'We will have to kill him. If we let him go, he will go to the police and we will get caught.' The die was cast. The decision was made.

'How much money do you have in your bank account?' Priya asked.

'Not much,' Dushyant replied in fear.

'Should we just take out everything he has in his account?' Dikshant suggested.

'You can't withdraw more than Rs 25,000 in a day. That's the withdrawal limit,' Dushyant didn't know which way his fate was headed.

'My father is sending the money. Please don't kill me. You will get your money. I will not complain to the police.' Dushyant tried to bargain for his breath. He had to strike a deal. 'I have an idea. I can get you the money. My father is paying you Rs 3 lakh. I can get you the balance Rs 7 lakh,' Dushyant was desperate.

'Again this is one of your useless attempts, like the cheque!' Dikshant retorted.

'No! No . . . let me call my friends. They will give the money,' Dushyant assured his captors.

Their greed got the better of them. *'Chal phone laga! Aur koi chutiyapa mat karna.'* (Start making the calls and no tricks.) Priya watched his every move.

According to Aravind Balakrishnan writing for the website Medium.com, Dushyant started calling his friends one by one, and each of them responded with the amount they could arrange.[45]

His friends asked him why he needed money so suddenly, and that too so early in the morning. All Dushyant could do was to keep inventing stories, one desperate lie after another to find redemption for the original lie of being Vivan.

'It is going to take time for him to collect the money from all of his friends. It makes no sense. And if we allow him to leave, this bastard will definitely return with the police. He knows where we live,' Priya finally said in a state of panic.

'We have to kill him.'

Priya was stupid. She was not thinking straight.

Let's study the situation. Imagine you are Priya, the abductor.

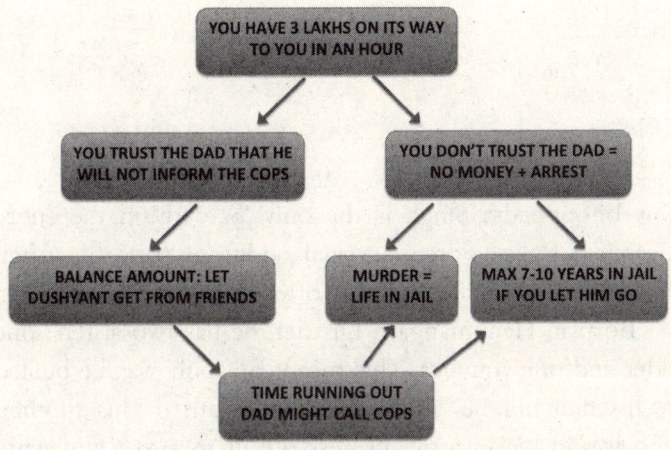

THIS IS WHERE WE ARE

To Kill or Not to Kill, that is the question.

Chapter Eleven

The First Step

Gur Bhoopendra Singh is the only 'Sardarji' in the entire Rajasthan Police Force: a visual oddity of sorts but often treated like a celebrity. Civilians often click pictures with him.

Born in Hanumangarh District, he has two sisters: one older and one younger. This meant not only was he bullied by his didi but he often faced the wrath of his mother, who would pick up the nearest object to strike him with. He became an expert at dodging. The reasons ranged from being naughty, to not completing his homework, to coming back home late after gallivanting around with friends. His didi also faced the missiles from their mother. The youngest, predictably was pampered.

'Kya banna hai?' (What do you want to be when you grow up?) the neighbour asked the twelve-year-old Gur.

'Engineer,' was the prompt reply.

'Tum toh sure lag rahe ho! Kyun banna hai engineer?' (You seem to be sure. But why do you want to be an engineer?)

'Mera maths achcha hai and my English is good! Aur mujhe Papa jaise engineer banna hai!' (I am good at Maths and English.

I want to be an engineer like my father.) Gur wanted to emulate his father. He was good in Math and English. And to the innocent twelve-year-old, the qualification was enough.

Gur Bhoopendra did his graduation from Hanumangarh District and came to the Pink City to pursue Bachelor of Laws. While studying law, he appeared for his first civil services exam, and he was selected. And so after completing his law, he got into the Indian Police Service (IPS) in December 1999. His father beamed with pride seeing his son as a police officer.

'Maine aur koi career ke bare mein socha hi nahi tha.' (I did not think of any other career.) Gur Bhoopendra recalled while speaking with me.

In 2004, Gur got a call from his mother. 'Can you come home?' she asked gingerly, not wanting to irritate Gur who was on duty.

Gur panicked, *'Sab changa si?'* (All okay?)

His mother assured him that all was fine and there was some good news. The plan was to arrange Gur and his younger sister's marriages at the same time. And the family had been looking for prospective brides and grooms for the both of them. Gur had been postponing the decision of getting married every year, using the workload as an excuse.

'We have found someone very nice. My heart tells me that you will like her,' Gur's mother told him over the phone. When she found no response, she tried to make him see reason. 'See, you will get married someday, so why delay the inevitable? If you get married when you are old, you won't be able to give your youth to your children. Do you want to play football with them while using a walking stick?'

Gur smiled at the other end. He knew his mother too well, and that she had a unique way of ensuring he saw the logic in what she was saying. *'Theek hai.* You tell me when to come.'

'Can you come day after?' Gur's mother was relieved her son had finally agreed to now meet the prospective bride.

Gur took leave for a day and headed back to Hanumangarh. He met Karamjeet and the two families chatted for half an hour, and both Gur and Karamjeet said yes to the union. And then Gur Bhoopendra Singh was off to do a commando course for the next three-and-a-half months.

In 2004, Karamjeet and Sub Inspector Gur Bhoopendra got married and three years later they were blessed with a daughter, Avinoor, and another two years later, a son, Yuvreet.

In 2011, Gur's father passed away and he dived straight into as much work as possible to keep the grief at bay.

In 2015, he earned a promotion and got posted to Jaipur.

'Karamjeet gets upset because I am not able to give her enough time. I am stuck at work for days. Because of work I always end up missing my son's birthday. Sometimes I wish I too could spend more time at home. I sometimes get a little jealous when I see how the kids are closer to their mom,' Gur Bhoopendra laughed as he confessed.

When the SHO (Station Head Officer), Father, Husband and Son Gur Bhoopendra Singh walked into the Jhotwara Police Station, he had no clue that a case was just minutes away from falling into his lap. A case that would shake him and bring tears to his eyes.

At approximately 10.30 a.m. a cousin of Dushyant's called up on the 100 Police Helpline to report a Missing Person, and a ransom threat, and left his own number. The control room called up Jhotwara Police Station. Gur Bhoopendra Singh picked up the call.

'Sir, we received a call on 100 about a missing man and his family had received a ransom call as well. And here is the number of the caller,' the control room shared the cousin's number.

Bhoopendra called back on the number and it was the cousin who picked up the phone and spoke to the inspector.

'Tell me in detail,' Gur Bhoopendra wanted to dive into the case right away.

'My cousin brother, his name is Dushyant. He left home yesterday in the evening saying that he had some urgent office work. But he didn't come back the whole night. This morning, his father got a call. Nikki . . . err . . . that is Dushyant's nickname. He sounded very worried and was crying on the phone saying they will kill me if we don't pay the ransom. Then a girl came on the line and demanded that Tauji pay a ransom of Rs 10 lakh in exchange for his son.'

'Okay, I am registering a first information report (FIR). I need to meet the father. Please share his number with me. Also, send me your cousin's photograph right away.'

The SHOs across Rajasthan have a WhatsApp group, where they share information regarding a case if they need help or leads from other regions of the state. There was a time when there were no computers or a central criminal digital database. And now with the help of technology, the SHOs or anyone can contact and exchange leads with others within seconds. Of course so do criminals.

As soon as Bhoopendra got Dushyant's photograph, he uploaded it on the WhatsApp group with the message: *New Case. Missing: Dushyant Sharma. Last seen yesterday at 7 p.m. Ransom call came in at 10 this morning. Keep me updated. Thanks.*

Gur Bhoopendra suddenly felt the hair rise on the back of his neck. He felt a sense of déjà vu as he sat down in his chair. His palms were sweaty.

In his head, he travelled back to December 2002 when he was a Sub Inspector posted in Jodhpur. A handicrafts trader's son by the name of Gaurav Jain had been kidnapped. It took the police nine days to solve the case and the search was spread across three states.[46] That was the biggest case of his career so far. This one was going to eclipse that in its notoriety, except Gur didn't know that yet.

Gur Bhoopendra Singh made another move. He put Dushyant's mobile number 8949604XXX on trace. The challenge is that the call list that's generated is not of the same day, but that of the previous day. So he got the call records of the 2nd.

He delegated work to his team. They were told to scan through the phone call list that had been generated of 2 May and check each number.

'Start checking the calls that happened after lunch, and the time of his disappearance.'

Gur Bhoopendra then formed his team. He called in Sub Inspector Maan Singh, Sub Inspector Hemant Janagal, and constables Suresh Bajiya and Praveen Poonia and debriefed them on the information he had at the moment. Maan Singh was an old-school cop. He was good at studying maps and clues and was very observant. Hemant on the other hand was enthusiasm personified. He was always on his toes and alert.

Gur Bhoopendra had worked with these two closely and knew they would have his back. He called the cousin's number and they decided to meet halfway.

Gur Bhoopendra instructed Sub Inspector Maan Singh and Sub Inspector Hemant to accompany him as the team headed out. He wanted everybody present for three reasons:

1. To avoid information being turned into a game of Chinese whisper. He wanted everybody on the team to have first-hand information
2. To save time and to avoid wastage of time in repeating the information
3. In a brand-new case, perspectives and insights are important, so he wanted his top team members to be present at the first meeting itself. Often, one officer misses something, which the other officer picks up on.

On the way, Bhoopendra called Rameshwar to assure him. 'Inspector saab, I have lost two of my three sons. Dushyant is the only son I have now. I don't want any harm to come to him. Please save him.' Rameshwar pleaded on the phone.

'Rameshwarji, I assure you we are on the case, and we are searching for your son.'

'Dushyant's cousin will help you out with all the information. You will have to excuse me as I am trying to arrange the money for the ransom. Once the work is done, I will contact you,' saying this Rameshwar disconnected.

'The number from which the ransom call was made—' before Bhoopendra could finish, the cousin piped in, 'It was from Nikki's own number 8949604XXX.' Gur Bhoopendra realized he was dealing with a seasoned criminal who knew how to hide their tracks. It was a delicate time in any hostage situation. The abductors had made a ransom demand, and a partial payout was happening.

He knew that from this point on, the events could go either way: the abductors could be greedy and wait for the rest of the money to get transferred, which would give the police team that many extra hours to investigate the case. Or the abductors could disappear with the initial amount and go incommunicado. The latter could put the hostage's fate in jeopardy.

Meanwhile, from the call records of the 2nd the police identified one number that had called Dushyant three times during the span of him leaving home to fifteen-odd minutes later. These were short calls, but they all came from one number: 8740988XXX. The number was registered to one Om Prakash. They tried the number, but it was switched off. They needed to track down Om Prakash!

Chapter Twelve

The Murder

We are now back at the moment where the trio will decide to either kill Dushyant or let him go.

If I was Priya, I would have let Dushyant go out to collect the money from his friends, but I would send Dikshant with him. Dushyant already had a car. Dikshant would accompany him and ensure he behaves. You see, they were not thinking straight. Panic had befuddled their brains.

Here is the scenario: Dushyant, accompanied by one of them, goes to pick up the money from his friends. At some point, he decides to act smart and drives to the police station, or even alerts his friends. The police would raid Eden Garden and arrest the kidnappers. This would entail a maximum jail term of seven to ten years for the trio.

But they opted for murder at this point. Priya was not only panicking, but her ego that was used to getting what she always wanted, had taken a huge beating as she had been outwitted by Dushyant. And the sociopath wanted revenge!

The decisive factor that sealed Dushyant's fate was that he lived in Jaipur. The trio was sure that in spite of Dushyant's sworn assurances that he would not squeal to the cops, there was a huge possibility he would. Had Dushyant truly been from New Delhi, he would have probably lived to see another day.

It was Friedrich Nietzsche who had said, 'I'm not upset that you lied to me, I'm upset that from now on I can't believe you.'[47] Well, Dushyant had definitely not read Nietzsche, but the trio of soon-to-be killers definitely knew what it felt to be taken for a ride, and it wasn't a happy or pleasant feeling. The panic-stricken, ego-battered, outwitted and vengeful Priya and Dikshant decided to kill him. And this was even before the first tranche of the ransom was transferred. They knew that Dushyant's father was arranging the money and yet without waiting for it, they had decided to kill Dushyant. Although Dikshant had feigned surprise when Priya had mentioned her ulterior plan to kill Dushyant, maybe they had both been prepared for it. Maybe they had hidden their intention from Lakshya whom they knew would freak out and panic. So, the ransom was just a ruse to give false hope to his parents, perhaps.

Dushyant swerved his head from side to side as Dikshant tried to put the polythene bag on his head and cover his face. He was thrown on the bed.

* * *

While the trio was mercilessly planning to kill Dushyant, Rameshwar was rushing to the bank. He was an accountant at a cooperative and did not earn much. So the Rs 3 lakh is all he had at the moment.

Rameshwar reached the Union Bank and met the manager, Rajender Kumar.

'I need to break the fixed deposit,' Rameshwar said.

As bank managers are prone to do, Rajender tried to hold on to the money and wanted to know why Rameshwar wanted to break the FD.

Rameshwar literally pleaded for the money to be transferred to his son's account urgently. Rajender realized there was something truly urgent about the situation and so he started the process assuring Rameshwar that it will be done in the next twenty minutes.

* * *

Dikshant climbed up on Dushyant's chest and tried to strangulate him with his bare hands. Dushyant fought back and thrashed about, trying to hang on to his life. Priya also joined in trying to throttle Dushyant. Dikshant looked like he was riding one of those mechanized rodeo bulls in the children's play area in the mall as Dushyant bucked about trying to throw Dikshant off his chest.

Seeing that this plan was not working, Priya brought a pillow from another room and handed it over to Lakshya, asking him to use it to suffocate Dushyant. Lakshya, too petrified to do it, handed over the pillow to Dikshant. Dikshant then placed the pillow on Dushyant's face and pressed hard. Dushyant's muffled groans could be heard emanating from inside the crackling polythene bag. Dushyant continued to fight back till the lack of oxygen made him black out and fall unconscious.

'Is he dead?' Priya asked expectantly.

Dikshant stared at Priya. Lakshya stared at Dikshant. It was a macabre tableau.

Dikshant slowly pulled the polythene bag from Dushyant's face and put his finger under his nostrils. He could feel the shallow, warm breath of life being exhaled from Dushyant. He was alive.

* * *

And this is where fifteen minutes turned into an hour. When Rameshwar gave Rajender the account number to which the money needed to get transferred, Rajender dropped a bomb. 'Rameshwarji, Dushyant's account does not have proper KYC. His Pan Card is not attached or updated to his account. We cannot transfer such a large sum of money to his account.'

Rameshwar could feel the world spinning around him. He sank in the chair. He argued saying, 'He is my son, this is my money and I am just transferring it to his account. What is the need for the Pan Card?'

Rajender uttered the two words we have gotten used to hearing for everything these days, 'Government regulations!'

'What is the solution?' Rameshwar screamed in panic. Time was ticking. He didn't want to lose his only son. While Rameshwar was desperately trying to ensure the transfer of the ransom, the trio had already begun the process of killing Dushyant. While Rameshwar clung on to hope, unknown to him fate had made her move.

'You need to go to the home branch that has Dushyant's account and get the Pan Card updated. Only then can we transfer the money,' Rajender insisted.

* * *

Priya rushed to the kitchen and returned with a fruit knife (5'x7') and handed it to Dikshant. Lakshya shrank back in fear. Dikshant held the knife in his hand. Priya looked at Dikshant. Their communication was clear.

'Both of you step back. Move away,' Dikshant said, turning to look at Dushyant, lying there helpless, unconscious, unable to fight back, not knowing that he was drawing his last breath. Dikshant took a deep breath, readied himself and then brought the knife down with brute force.

Khach!! The blade of the knife dug itself in Dushyant's throat. As Dikshant pulled the knife out, a crimson fountain burst forth from the wound, drenching Dushyant and the bed. The white, green and red coloured bed sheet started soaking up the blood like a hungry demon.

Khach!! Dikshant again brought the knife down. It entered his thorax and blood spurted out hitting Dikshant on the face. His face looked like he had been playing Holi.

Khach!! Khach!! Khach!!! Dikshant repeatedly brought the knife down on Dushyant's neck, mauling it. Dushyant's body convulsed as the brain registered the trauma and the attack. But Dushyant did not awaken.

Khach!! Khach!! The bed and the floor had turned into a pool of blood as the seven-inch blade of the knife repeatedly entered into the soft flesh of Dushyant's neck and exited like a knife cutting through a cake.

And Dikshant did not stop even though Dushyant was dead. He wanted to ensure that Dushyant would never come back.

Khach! Khach!! Khach!!!

Ten stab wounds in the neck. And Dushyant was finally dead.

Dikshant was panting. He turned his bloodied face to
look at Priya. Lakshya stood there not fully comprehending
what had just happened and its consequences.

'You go home and change your clothes. Stay there till
we tell you what to do,' Dikshant instructed Lakshya Walia,
who scampered off to his Malviya Nagar house.

'We need to clean this mess,' Priya said.

Dikshant got off from his seated position atop Dushyant's
chest. As Dikshant stood up, drops of blood from his clothes
dripped on to the floor, as if he had entered the house after
being drenched in the rain. As if Dikshant had embodied
the twelfth-century poet Layamon's poem 'Brut' (written
around 1190):

'From heaven here came a marvelous flood; three days it
rained blood, three days and three nights.'

* * *

Rameshwar did not have a picture of Dushyant's Pan Card
on his phone. And he knew going back home to get it was
not an option as Dushyant always carried it with him in his
wallet. So he dialled Dushyant's number.

* * *

Just then Dushyant's mobile started ringing. The screen
displayed 'Papa'.

Dikshant and Priya looked at each other, their hearts
skipping a beat. They panned their heads from the phone to
the bloody corpse lying on the bed. Priya knew if they didn't
pick up the phone, the father could get suspicious and then

alert the police. So Priya picked up the phone to go along with the script she had written.

In her brusque manner she spoke into the phone, *'Kya hua? Kya chahiye? Paise kahan hai?'* (What happened? What do you want? Where's the money?)

'Paise mil jayengay. Ek problem ho gaya hai!' (You will get the money. But there has been a problem.) Rameshwar stammered in nervousness.

Priya immediately started berating Rameshwar and accused him of trying to cheat them and buy more time.

'Believe me, the bank officer told me that Dushyant's account does not have a Pan Card attached and without that the money cannot get transferred,' Rameshwar tried to make his case heard, 'Please give the phone to Dushyant. Let me speak with him.'

As Dushyant lay dead on the bed, his blood slowly congealing on his clothes and on the bed, Priya realized their game could be up right at that moment. Also being a cheat and criminal herself, she suspected Rameshwar of lying about the Pan Card fiasco as a ruse to speak with his son. She decided to go on the offensive.

'You are lying to us,' She screamed over the phone. 'You are simply buying more time. Have you informed the police?'

Rameshwar panicked, 'No, No. I have not told the police anything. I am not lying. I am telling you the truth. Please believe me. Please speak to the bank manager if you don't believe me.'

Rameshwar thrust the phone at Rajender Kumar, the bank manager, who suddenly found himself in the middle of a hostage situation, even though at that time he did not know it. 'Rameshwarji is not lying. He is telling the truth. Dushyant's account does not a Pan Card attached, and without that we cannot transfer the money to his account.' Rajender laid out the facts.

'Okay. Dushyant will send you the Pan Card number,' saying this, she disconnected the phone.

'Now what?' Dikshant asked in panic.

'We will send him the Pan Card number. Where is his wallet? His Pan Card was in the wallet,' saying this Priya and Dikshant searched for the wallet. They retrieved his wallet and took out Dushyant's Pan Card. She quickly took a photo of it on Dushyant's phone and sent it to 'Papa' Rameshwar.

Rameshwar then journeyed towards Dushyant's State Bank of India 'home branch' to make the transfer.

In the meanwhile, Dikshant and Priya started cleaning up the flat as best as they could. They wiped the floor with a cloth mop. The mop was dripping with the congealed blood. Priya's designer shoes were stained with Dushyant's blood. The duo shoved Dushyant's pair of blood-splattered white sneakers hurriedly under the bed.

They used whatever they could get their hands on to try and clean up the cruor.

An old used double bed sheet in red, blue and yellow colour, a small netted tablecloth of plastic, a sheet of designer wallpaper and a plastic transparent floral printed tablecloth were all used to soak up the blood.

Chapter Thirteen

The Cover-Up

Dikshant's trousers was drenched with Dushyant's blood. There was a metallic smell in the room. 'We need to get rid of the body' was the only thought both of them were nurturing at that point.

The magnitude of what they had done had not hit them yet. In a matter of a few seconds, they had gone from being con artists to kidnappers to cold-blooded killers. In a matter of minutes, they had sacrificed their lives of freedom for incarceration forever.

Dikshant's trouser was sticking to his leg. The blood had started making the pant feel as if it had been starched. Dikshant changed his clothes. He shoved his blood-soaked jeans and shirt under the mattress of the bed. And after discussion with Priya, the decision was made to get a suitcase into which they would stuff Dushyant's body and dump it somewhere remote. They took the car keys from Dushyant, along with his phone and ATM card.

They locked the flat with Dushyant's body in it, lying on the bed, lifeless and with rigor mortis slowly setting in.

They came down to the parking area and got into Dushyant's Hyundai i-10 and headed towards Sodala. They made the approximate 6.6 km journey to buy the suitcase. The decision to buy it from a shop located at a distance was to avoid raising suspicion or leaving a trail close to the scene of crime. They parked the car and searched for a shop selling suitcases. This was at around 11.45 a.m.

Kamal Meghani Baig saw a boy and a girl walk into his store. They wanted to buy a bag. 'What size are you looking at?' Kamal Meghani asked.

In her head, Priya thought, 'Large enough to fit a dead body' but she mumbled, 'A large bag. A trolley bag.'

'Yeh trolley bag solid hai. Koralite brand ka hai.' (This bag is sturdy. It's Koralite.) The shopkeeper showed them a purple trolley bag.

The duo bought a big-size green tarpaulin bag for Rs 400 and the purple trolley bag for Rs 1600. The irony was the trolley bag that was being purchased by Dushyant's card was soon going to become a coffin for him. The duo loaded both the bags in the car and headed back towards Anita Nagar. Just then, an alert pinged on Dushyant's mobile.

Priya studied the screen for a few seconds before a smile appeared on her face. The SMS alert was from the bank stating that Rs 3 lakh had been deposited into Dushyant's account. But Priya was not happy as her demand of Rs 10 lakh had not been met.

Her greed, obstinacy, impatience and sense of entitlement were supreme. Used to getting what she wanted, she always needed to have control and the upper hand in any situation. Unfortunately, at the moment things were not under her control. And she hated it.

'What will happen if and when the father pays the full amount?' There was a tinge of panic in Dikshant's voice. 'How will we . . .' He let his voice trail off, knowing fully well that returning the son in exchange for the ransom was no longer a viable option.

The plan was clear. They would dump Dushyant's body as quickly as possible.

Just then Dushyant's phone rang.

By 12 p.m., Rameshwar, who had managed to transfer Rs 3 lakh to Dushyant's savings account with the State Bank of India, was now calling up to inform the abductors. He even clicked a photo of the receipt for the transaction and sent it to Dushyant's phone via WhatsApp.

Priya picked up the call.

'Maine Rs 3 lakh transfer kar diya!' Rameshwar said, *'Aur Rs 7 lakh, aaj shaam tak transfer kar dunga!'* (I have transferred Rs 3 lakh and I will transfer the remaining Rs 7 lakh by this evening.)

Priya was her usual brusque, pampered, psychotic self and wanted her new toy right there and then, *'Abhi kar transfer! Rs 7 lakh mujhe abhi chahiye!'* (Do the transfer now. I want the Rs 7 lakh now!) saying this she disconnected the phone.

'Let's withdraw the money,' Priya suggested to Dikshant and then she wrapped a dupatta around her head and face before entering a State Bank of India ATM in Bajaj Nagar. She inserted Dushyant's ATM card into the machine and typed in the pin. She typed out the amount to withdraw. But to her consternation, the ATM informed her that the daily withdrawal limit was Rs 25,000. She cursed under her breath as she remembered Dushyant informing them about the same the previous night. Dushyant wasn't alive any more for her to force him to log on to the bank website and change the withdrawal limit. She withdrew the Rs 25,000 in three transactions. Then, Dikshant and Priya drove back home. And then Dushyant's phone was switched off.

The police team started calling up Dushyant's friends and colleagues trying to form an information picture of WHAT had triggered this incident, WHO was behind this and WHY did they do it. Was there any other motive other than money?

The thought kept niggling Gur Bhoopendra. Why was their son kidnapped in spite of the family being middle class with no assets or money? Something wasn't fitting. The motive was a layered one. And the perpetrator could be someone Dushyant knew well.

The WHEN and HOW was already an approximation. Bhoopendra had started piecing the puzzles together. Dushyant was in all probability lured out of the house by a phone call from the phone number registered under the name of Om Prakash at 7 p.m. The constables were sent off to Dushyant's office to check whether Om Prakash worked there or was one of their vendors or if somebody could give a lead.

While speaking to one friend, a clue emerged. Parikh, Dushyant's friend, mentioned that Dushyant was having an affair with a girl from Bajaj Nagar. And another friend made a sarcastic and a cryptic comment saying, 'A twenty-five–twenty-six-year-old man doesn't disappear on his own (without a motive).' These two clues were now beginning to create an insight into the motive.

In his experience, Bhoopendra had come across cases where the victim has planned the abduction to get money from their own family. And because a woman made the ransom call, Bhoopendra, for a moment, thought that maybe

Dushyant being young, was now executing the kidnap-and-ransom plan in tandem with his lover from Bajaj Nagar. He was partially right. Dushyant had in fact been having an affair of sorts with Priya. But the rest of the assumption was far from the truth.

Bhoopendra put a notice out to look out for Dushyant's white i-10.

'Hemant and Maan Singh, get in touch with all the informers you have. Tell them we are looking for the car in and around Bajaj Nagar. And ask them to call you back as soon as they spot it.'

The two sub inspectors immediately set the plan in motion. They passed on the vehicle registration number, make, colour and the area where it was likely to be spotted. The informants of the police force are like Sherlock Holmes's Baker Street Irregulars, who are a bunch of street boys employed by Holmes as intelligence agents. According to Holmes, they are able to 'go everywhere and hear everything'. And this is exactly what Bhoopendra was expecting of the *khabris* of Jaipur.

* * *

I have transferred the amount. Now why aren't they responding? Rameshwar was worried.

This was conveyed to Bhoopendra who cursed under his breath. Having worked on cases of abduction, he knew this could mean two things: either the abductors were scared, gotten spooked and gone inside their holes, which was bad news, because when abductors are scared they are prone to do stupid things, like kill their victims or go on the run with them. Or at this point, hopefully they would once again emerge out of their hole to withdraw the money and establish contact if they were greedy for the balance amount.

But till these two things happened, all Bhoopendra and his team could do was to keep looking for the car and go through the call list. He asked Rameshwar to inform the bank manager to alert them if any transactions occurred from Dushyant's bank account. The manager was to tell them immediately. Gur Bhoopendra knew one thing for sure: that the ransom was the worm at the end of the fishing line that would bring the fish to the surface. They would withdraw the money and that would give him and his team a breadcrumb to follow.

Chapter Fourteen

The Disposal of the Body

When the duo returned to 402 Eden Garden, Bajaj Nagar, the plan was clear in their heads. They would stuff the body into the trolley bag and then dispose it off in a secluded spot.

Had the twenty-seven-year-old Priya remembered the ghastly case of Maria Susairaj and her lover Jerome killing Neeraj Grover, as she had seen the case unfold when she was seven years old? Maria and Jerome had taken the dead body to the kitchen and chopped it into several pieces, stuffing them into the bags Susairaj had earlier bought.

Dikshant and Priya didn't have the stomach to chop the body. They only wanted to pack the body into the bag. Dikshant first tried putting the body in the plastic bag. He found it tough. A dead body becomes heavy, it is dead weight, and it also does not cooperate with you. Although it is lifeless, it seems to still have a mind of its own as the arms flay around, the legs don't stand up, the head lolls back. It is like trying to control a giant puppet, except you do not have the strings. Dikshant broke out into a rush of sweat. This was hard work.

He somehow managed to stuff the body into the large plastic bag, but it tore from one side. The plastic bag was to ensure the blood does not soak through the trolley bag. The plan had to be abandoned. Along with Priya, they now struggled to get the body into the purple trolley bag.

Rigor mortis was slowly setting in and the body had begun to stiffen. They first took off the numerous astrological rings and red and black threaded amulets that Dushyant was wearing. They stuffed these into the inside pocket of the bag.

'Where do we dump him?' Dikshant asked as both of them heaved and sweated as they carried the corpse and placed it inside the trolley bag.

'Near Le Meridien. I know that area very well,' Priya said as the duo now stood up and stared at Dushyant lying in the trolley bag, spread-eagled.

The legs and arms were popping out. They turned Dushyant to his side and then manipulated the lifeless body into a foetal position. By doing this, they were able to fit the body into the trolley bag. The head was placed at an odd angle. The duo stuffed two pieces of saree and dupatta under the head to prop it up and Dikshant zipped up the trolley bag.

The two lovers looked at each other in satisfaction. Stage 2 of their plan to dispose of the body was now in process.

Dikshant put the trolley bag upright and the body shifted inside. The startled Dikshant let go of the handle for a second.

He swallowed hard and wheeled out the trolley bag from 402 to the lift. If someone had spotted him with the trolley bag, it would look like Dikshant was off to catch a flight— like a casual traveller who would soon update his Facebook status as *'Excited at Sanganer Airport.'* But this was a far cry from normalcy and the usual, everyday travel packing.

Dikshant pressed the button to call the lift. Somewhere below, it whirred to life, and started travelling up to the fourth floor. The lift was taking a long time to come. Dikshant prayed for the lift to be empty. He kept looking over his shoulder every now and then, hoping the neighbours wouldn't pop out of nowhere. The ding of the lift startled him as it announced its arrival. Dikshant wheeled the trolley bag into the lift. Priya who was standing outside the door of their apartment, now locked the door and signalled Dikshant to go ahead in the lift, while she took the stairs.

Dikshant took the lift, while Priya took the stairs. Why did they travel separately from the flat to the parking?

Was Priya scared to travel in the lift with the corpse? Was she apprehensive of getting caught and therefore did not want to take chances? Was it a masterstroke on her part to let Dikshant accompany the corpse so that if he got caught, she could just disown him and walk away leaving him alone?

Dikshant exited the lift and headed towards the parking area on the ground floor. He supported the heavy trolley bag by leaning it against the wall near the door of the lift. He got into Dushyant's car and reversed it, bringing it closer to the lift. Bhagwan, one of the security men for the building, was having his food when he noticed Dikshant reversing the car towards the lift. Shyam Sundar Sharma, the other guard, said, *'Bhaiya, wahan parking mat kijiye.'* (Don't park there.)

Dikshant got out of the driver's seat, *'Heavy suitcase hain. Load karke hum nikal jayengay.'* (It's a heavy suitcase. We will load it into the car and leave.)

The bag was too heavy for them to be lifting in front of the security guards. They wanted to be as discreet as possible. Both of them had to use their muscle power to lift the trolley bag and place it in the dicky[48] of the car.

Dikshant turned to Shyam Sundar and told him, 'We are going out. When the cook comes, tell her she does not need to cook today.'

Less than twenty-four hours ago, Dushyant had been all excited as he drove his car into Eden Garden thinking he was going to have a romantic one-night stand. And here he was now: dead, stuffed in a trolley bag.

The car drove out of Eden Garden on a mission.

Many of the media houses, newspapers and TV channels in their effort to gain eyeballs, TRPs and attention added much spice to the story. Their agenda was simple: the more gruesome they made it out to be, the higher the ratings. And so there were reports of the duo chopping up the body and packing it up piece by piece. The reality however was that Dushyant's body was not chopped up.

When I asked the same question to SHO Bhoopendra Singh he said the body was intact when they took it out of the trolley bag.

The duo had called up Lakshya and instructed him to come at Nandpuri Underpass.

Earlier, Lakshya had gone back home to Malviya Nagar, completely shaken by what he had witnessed a few hours ago. Never in his life did he think he would see someone getting stabbed and murdered right in front of his eyes. He was witness to a cold-blooded murder. And that was not all, now he was an accomplice too. The thought of it almost made him shit his pants. On receiving the call from Priya and Dikshant, the trepidation he had experienced returned to shake him up.

He took an auto for the five-minute ride from his house to the underpass and waited there for the duo to join him. Within minutes, the Hyundai i-10 reached the destination.

'Get in! We don't have time. Hurry,' Priya instructed.

Lakshya got into the car and gingerly took the back seat.

'Where is it?' he whispered.

'Dicky' was the one-word answer elicited by Dikshant.

As his back touched the seat, Lakshya felt a shiver go down his spine. He knew very well what was behind him. One of them joked, 'Don't be scared, he is not going to pop out of the trolley bag and attack.' The trio then drove off to get rid of the body.

While Dikshant drove, Priya searched for a secluded spot in Kukas village near Le Méridien on Google maps on her phone. She was familiar with the area. She knew it would be secluded, and hence easy for them to dump the body.

While on the way, they realized that they were running low on petrol.

What if the car stalled and they were stuck with the corpse? Or they could just abandon the car and run away? Different thoughts raced through Dikshant's mind as he scanned the sides of the road for a petrol pump.

They drove into the Shaheed Bastiram Filling Station on the Jhalana Bypass at 2.30 p.m. and purchased petrol worth Rs 500.

After filling petrol they drove towards Khor Gate near the Delhi highway. The silence in the car was rife with tension. They were no longer joking. The gnawing tension ate at them. They knew that only once the trolley bag was dumped would they be separated from the crime and the evidence. And it would signal the end of this bloody, sordid saga. And so, although they were a few kilometers away from the Le Meridien area, they decided to get rid of the body pronto!

At approximately 3 p.m., as they neared Khor Darwaza, they stopped the car when they spotted a desolate spot. The two men quickly got out of the car and looked around. There was no one in sight. They quickly flipped open the dicky of the hatchback and lifted the trolley bag out. They looked around once more, just to make sure nobody was watching them. Then they lowered the trolley bag on the side of the road and sprung back into the car. They had managed to get rid of the evidence, but they were still stressed out. They slammed on the accelerator and sped off. They wanted to put as much distance as possible between them and the evidence, and as fast as possible.

On the way back, Dikshant had a masterstroke. 'Even if the police are searching for Dushyant's car, they will be searching for it by the number. We will get a fake number plate. That way, we will be able to roam around freely.'

And so Dikshant bought a fake number plate RJ14AQ 4384 from a shop owned by Shri Suryaprakash opposite the petrol pump, in exchange for a copy of his Aadhaar card. Dikshant kept the number plate in the car. 'We will use it later, when we need to.'

When the car turned towards Sodala, instead of Bajaj Nagar, Lakshya queried, 'Why are we not going home? Why to Sodala?'

'We need to buy another trolley bag,' Priya said coldly.

At this point, the thought of Priya and Dikshant eliminating him next and stuffing him in the trolley bag must have crossed Lakshya's mind. After all, they were lovers and he was the thorn, the witness, the accomplice, and the one who was most likely to squeal.

'Why?' Lakshya asked nervously.

'Because we went out of the house with a trolley bag, and we need to return with the same trolley bag.'

The three of them drove back to the shop at Sanganer Road, Sodala. The owner, Kamal Meghani, was surprised to see the girl and the boy walk in again. He recognized the girl. This was at approximately 4.30 p.m. Priya and Dikshant asked for a similar trolley bag like the one they had bought earlier. They did not want any other colour, but the exact same purple one.

This was also done perhaps keeping the Maria Susairaj case in mind, where the building watchman had seen Maria and Emile Jerome Mathew exit the building with a suitcase but return empty-handed.

Priya and Dikshant then dropped Lakshya at his Malviya Nagar residence and themselves returned to Eden Garden. Lakshya felt a sense of relief.

* * *

Gur Bhoopendra Singh, the SHO of Jhotwara Police Station (Jaipur) was studying the call records of Dushyant when he noticed that there were multiple outgoing calls made within an hour. He knew he would find a clue hidden in these outgoing calls.

He instructed his team members to call back each of the numbers that Dushyant had called. The numbers turned out to be Dushyant's friends and they all had the same story: that Dushyant had called them just a few hours ago asking for money.

Bhoopendra pieced the timeline and the sequence of events. These phone calls were made after Rameshwar had promised to transfer the Rs 3 lakh and he had informed the kidnappers that the transfer had been made. The SHO figured out that Dushyant would have been desperate to save his own life, as he knew the reality of the situation at home. His father could not have afforded to pay the rest of the ransom. But one question kept niggling him: why was a middle-class person like Dushyant kidnapped for ransom? He was a simple man, and the family did not have any enemies. *The sand mafia!* The SHO suddenly had a eureka moment.

Was it their doing? And more importantly if it was indeed the mafia, why was a woman making the ransom call? The mafia wasn't of a disputatious (I had to look this one up) nature. They hated conversations, they just killed.

And so as quickly as the thought had occurred to Bhoopendra, the faster it dissipated into the ether. There was something else happening here. Inspector Bhoopendra was well aware of the 'honey trap' and 'blackmail' gangs that had suddenly sprung up in Jaipur as a business model to earn a quick buck in the promise of a quick fuck. And this case reeked of the same modus operandi.

He now was sure Dushyant had not orchestrated his kidnapping in the hope of fleecing his own family.

* * *

In the meanwhile, the duo parked the car at a safe distance from the house. Without any hesitation, Priya cleaned herself up and went in the direction of The Hilton the same evening to continue her 'escort service-con job' drama, unfazed by the fact that she had brutally murdered an innocent man just a few hours ago. Like a well-oiled machine, the proven-and-tested modus operandi was executed. She reached the hotel, collected her payment, asked the customer to wait till she paid the driver and left the hotel. She was completely unflurried by the fact that she had just disposed of a dead body.

By the time Priya came back with her earnings, Dikshant had tidied up the house as much as he could.

Chapter Fifteen

The Body Is Discovered

Amer SHO Inspector Narendra Choudhury received a call.

'Sir, there is a large trolley bag lying near Khor Darwaza,' the caller informed. Khor Darwaza was under the Amer Police Station's jurisdiction.

The year 2017 had seen a record-breaking 47.53 million tourists descend upon Rajasthan.[49] And 2018 already had gotten off to a great start. Choudhury knew that a large, stray trolley bag could be the harbinger of trouble if it turned out to be a bomb. It would project Rajasthan as an unsafe tourist destination. And that is something he wanted to avoid at all cost. Narendra called up the bomb squad and they headed to the area. He was the first person to reach the site.

The trolley bag was opened with much care and dexterity by the bomb squad. Immediately, a fetid smell assaulted their nostrils and they stepped back. The squad immediately recognized the smell. It was a corpse.

The body was curled up and stuffed in the purple trolley bag, as if the boy was feeling cold and had hugged his knees in the foetal position to stay warm. The body was bare-footed. Narendra clicked a couple of photographs of the corpse on his mobile phone. He then uploaded them on the WhatsApp group for the SHOs saying; 'A dead boy has been found. Does anybody have any information?' Simultaneously, the control room of the North District Commissionerate sent out the same message via the wireless to all the police stations in the city.

The body was then transported to the mortuary at Sawai Man Singh (SMS) Hospital. The Amer Police Station in-charge Mukesh Kumar completed the paperwork and the processes to keep the body at SMS Hospital.

Bhoopendra lost all hope as he stared at the picture of the dead body on the WhatsApp group for SHOs. He knew that this was Dushyant. For the police working on cases of abduction, it is hope and optimism that fuels their determination to find the victim and to chase the case. They subconsciously manifest and visualize the rescue of the victim. And it is that positive image that keeps pushing them one step at a time. And now, Bhoopendra was staring at the body of the man that he had hoped to rescue.

The inspector showed the photos to Dushyant's family, who immediately recognized the victim to be Dushyant. The parents broke down. They were inconsolable. All the hope and prayers were now in vain. Receiving a positive ID on the body, Bhoopendra informed the Amer Station in-charge Mukesh Kumar that the body belonged to a case registered at the Jhotwara Police Station. Mukesh informed Bhoopendra that the body was now at SMS Hospital.

Identifying via a photograph was just the preliminary step. The identification needed to be done physically. And so

Bhoopendra took the family to the hospital. The body was lifted out of the trolley bag and was placed in the ambulance. Bhoopendra took a look at the body. It was maimed and mutilated. The killer had brutally slashed the victim's throat several times. Gur advised Rameshwar, the victim's father, to not see the body. It was Dushyant's cousin who stepped forward to identify the body.

Rameshwar wailed, 'I have lost everything in my life. God, why did you snatch my last son from me?' And he fainted with grief.

Seeing a parent losing his last surviving child, Bhoopendra could feel his stomach tighten and his eyes were smarting from the grief. In the line of duty, the police are taught to control their emotions and not display them. Bhoopendra was a tough cop, but he could not hold his tears back this time. He was a father too and he could empathize with what the father was going through. Every time Bhoopendra saw a parent lose a child, he could relate to the pain. And then he harnessed this emotion to push himself to get justice for the victim.

And here Rameshwar had lost all three of his children to mishaps. Bhoopendra clenched his jaw—a surge of determination flooded through him. He knew he had to catch the killer to bring closure to Rameshwar.

When I asked him how he reacts to such heinous crimes, SHO Bhoopendra sat silently for a few seconds, lost in his thoughts, and then replied, 'As a parent, I feel insecure about the world my child is growing up in. I see crimes every day. I sometimes wonder what kind of a world we are bringing our kids into.'

'Can I take my son home?' Rameshwar asked had once he recovered.

'Sir, we will be conducting a post-mortem examination. I am afraid you cannot take back the . . .' At this point, Bhoopendra checked himself, it is normal to say 'body' for a dead person, he didn't like that word. 'Sir, you cannot take back Dushyant home today. There are police formalities and procedures that need to be followed.'

Bhoopendra, who was the investigating officer of the case, prepared the documents pertaining to the identification of Dushyant. The devastated family left for their home as Dushyant's body was shifted from the SMS Hospital to the Kanwatia Hospital for the post-mortem. The first charge that was added to the case was IPC Section 302,[50] as prima facie it looked like a case of murder.

While searching the trolley bag for clues and evidence, the police found two blood-soaked pieces of sari and a dupatta, one of which was knotted. From the top pocket of the bag, they recovered red and black threaded amulet and astrological rings.

The purple Koralite bag was then wrapped in a white bag and marked as Exhibit A-1—the first official piece of evidence in the Jaipur Tinder Murder Case. The pieces of the sari and dupatta were packed as Exhibit A-2. The amulets and the rings were wrapped up and marked as Exhibit A-3.

Back at the location where the body had been found, the area was cordoned off. But since it was late night and dark, the spot could not be mapped. The forensics and the police team had to physically map the crime scene. This means walking around, observing the place, looking for clues, picking up objects that are found there and in the vicinity like cigarette butts, papers, blood, shoeprints etc. As it was night, the team did not want to map the crime scene lest they accidentally tread on any 'evidence.'

The order to form a medical board for the post-mortem was acquired from the Commissioner of Police, Jaipur (West), which was handed over to the director of the Kanwatia Hospital.

The *panchayatnama* or *panchnama* process or the inquest for the body was done before the medical board performed the post-mortem.

In ancient India's judicial system, and even now at the village level, justice was and is administered by a group of five elected village 'seniors' known as 'Panch'. This process was documented as 'Panchanama', referring to the written record of the proceedings before the Panch. This term later extended to a document created by investigating officers to record investigation facts and progress.

This entails the police inviting random, unconnected (to the crime, criminal or the victim) eyewitnesses or *'panchas'* to observe the 'mapping' as the police collect evidence from the scene of crime. The police then record the statements of these eyewitnesses as corroboration, so that in the court of law the accused will not be able to contest the evidence as being planted.

In this case, two types of Panchnamas are drawn up:

1. The 'Spot' Panchnama: The investigating officer creates a sketch at the crime scene, documenting details witnessed by both the IO and panchas (witnesses). This includes descriptions of the location's size, whether it's isolated or open, like a room or public area. The arrangement of objects is noted. For murder cases, this involves the victim's position, weapon placement, other items present, the condition of the room and lighting.

These details aid in cross-examining Pancha Witnesses for effective corroboration.

2. Inquest Panchanama: The inquest panchanama is conducted according to Section 174 of the Code of Criminal Procedure, commonly called Criminal Procedure Code, when someone dies under suspicious circumstances like suicide, murder or accident. This process involves documenting details such as the position of the body, any injuries present and potential causes of death. The aim is to determine if the death appears to be unnatural based on initial observations of the body.

In our murder case, the clothes worn by Dushyant were soaked in his blood. He was in a pair of jeans and T-shirt, which were procured as evidence and were kept in a white bag, shielded and marked as Exhibit-B. The post-mortem was conducted on Dushyant's body. After the examination, the body was handed over to his family for cremation.

Rameshwar broke down when he was handed the red and black threaded amulet and the astrological gemstone rings. These were meant to protect his son and yet there was his son gone much before his time. Death and misfortune had claimed his third son too.

Now with one of the main elements of the case—the retrieval of the body—closed, the major part remained: to track down the criminals. Bhoopendra felt a rage surging inside him when he saw the way Dushyant was stuffed into a bag. It was heinous. And the SHO was determined to track down the murderers.

* * *

Meanwhile, Priya and Dikshant bathed, ordered pizza, ate and fell asleep promptly as the adrenaline that had been coursing their veins now waned, and exhaustion took over.

This would prove to be an expensive mistake, as you will discover later.

Chapter Sixteen

The Morning After

The night had been rough for Bhoopendra. He was in bed twisting and turning, unable to get any sleep. He wanted the night to end so that he could go back to where the body was found. He wanted to hunt for clues, scouring through every inch of space. All he could see was Dushyant's body curled up in a foetal position inside the purple bag. All he could see was Rameshwar breaking down on seeing the mutilated body of his son. All the inspector wanted to do was nab the murderer/s and put them behind bars.

Meanwhile, at Eden Garden, the duo of Dikshant and Priya woke up with a sense of trepidation. Dikshant's mind was in turmoil. His mind was hazy. Having given countless auditions for movie roles in Aram Nagar, Versova in Mumbai —which is where most casting directors of the film and television industry are located—Dikshant felt like he had just auditioned for the role of a murderer. Everything felt very unreal, like being in a film.

But when he looked at the blood-soaked bed on which he had stabbed Dushyant just a day before, he realized that he had not given an audition, nor did the murder happen in a movie scene—but it was for real—and that he was one of the killers!

* * *

As soon as day broke, Bhoopendra and his team reached the area at Khor Darwaza and mapped out the area, carefully searching for clues. Much to his disappointment, there was nothing to be found. The sun was now beginning to beat down upon them. They could feel the beads of sweat trickle down their spines and settle at the small of their backs.

* * *

Back at Eden Garden the trio sat down to chart out the next steps as they threw possibilities into the hat.

'What do we do?'

'We wait and watch.'

'We stay back for four to five days and we keep withdrawing Rs 25,000 every day till we have extracted the Rs 3 lakh.'

'That's twelve days!'

'Maybe we should try to get out of here.'

'And go where?'

'Why should I escape? I am doing my BCom here and I don't want to ruin my education!' Lakshya argued petulantly.

'The police would have started searching for Dushyant. Do you think they will trace his footsteps to us?'

This set off a panic amongst the ranks. The trio hurriedly locked up the flat and went down the lift. They were not able to think straight. They didn't utter a single word to each other as all of them were preoccupied in their own thoughts. They now found themselves in very unfamiliar waters.

'Just walk towards the car and get in. Don't act suspicious. Act normal.' These were the directives discussed upstairs, before they decided to step out into the sun from their cave of crime.

They walked towards Dushyant's Hyundai i-10 and quietly slipped in, trying their best to act normal so as not to attract attention. They looked around to ensure no one was watching.

'Now what?' Dushyant asked, once they were in the car.

There was no answer. Just silence. Nobody knew what to do next?

* * *

The police had instructed the bank manager of Dushyant's home branch to alert them if any transactions were made from his account. As he was going through Dushyant's bank statement, the manager noticed the code for three ATM withdrawals totalling to the daily limit of Rs 25,000. The withdrawals had been done within minutes of each other and at the same ATM. The manager copied down the code of the ATM from which the money had been extracted. It was an ATM in the Bajaj Nagar area. He immediately called up Rameshwar. A relative answered the phone. His eyes lit up when he heard the news.

Rameshwar asked, '*Kya hua?*' (What is it?)

'*Saalon ne koi ATM se Rs 25,000 withdrawal kiya hai. Inspector ne kaha tha unhe inform karne ke liye!*' (The bastards have withdrawn Rs 25,000 from an ATM. The inspector had asked us to keep him informed.)

The bank manager dialled Gur Bhoopendra's number.

Gur Bhoopendra and his team were at the hospital when the call came in. The post-mortem was almost done. The SHO picked up the call and listened intently. The bank manager informed him about the money being withdrawn. The IO knew that they were already running close to twelve hours behind the footsteps of the criminals and the crime. He told the relative to inform the bank to keep a watch on the account.

As they stood outside the hospital, Bhoopendra got a message from one of his informers. He had spotted the white i-10 with the license plate RJ14AC2555 near the Gandhinagar station in Bajaj Nagar, with people sitting inside it.

One of the skills an IO needs to develop is the ability to join the dots at the right time, to recall minute details that nobody thinks is important and to read between the lines.

At the mention of Bajaj Nagar, Bhoopendra suddenly had a brainwave. He remembered Parikh, Dushyant's friend, mentioning that Dushyant was in a relationship with a girl from Bajaj Nagar. And that's when the missing piece to the puzzle was found.

Why was a middle-class boy like Dushyant kidnapped for a ransom?

The answer was: he had been honey-trapped. Except it had gone horribly wrong when the victim's family could not pay the entire ransom amount. Or maybe their relationship had turned sour and the girl now wanted revenge!

Without wasting a moment, Bhoopendra and his team headed towards Bajaj Nagar.

This could go either way:

1. The killers could wait and keep coming out of their hiding, withdrawing Rs 25,000 per day for the next eleven days to withdraw the total ransom money; or
2. Having realized the account had a daily withdrawal limit of Rs 25,000 the killers were now making one last withdrawal before fleeing.

Bhoopendra did not know which way the tide would turn.

The Gandhinagar Railway Station is one of the two main stations of Jaipur. It is located in Bajaj Nagar area of the city and many trains to and from Delhi, Ghaziabad, Haridwar, Gurgaon and Ajmer have a stoppage at this station.

Just a few months ago, on 20 February 2018, the Gandhinagar Station had become the first all-women's operated railway station in India. From the ticket checkers, Railway Police Force and operations staff to the reservation and booking supervisors, twenty-eight women employees were handling the station.

Bhoopendra was driving his own car instead of the official vehicle. He did not want to spook the criminals. He was the only one in uniform. He was accompanied by sub-inspectors Maan Singh and Hemant, as well as three constables Suresh, Praveen and Suman (a lady constable). ACP Aash Mohammed joined them too. All of them were in mufti.

'Keep a look out for Dushyant's white i-10 with plate RJ14AC2555. The informer has seen the car with people sitting inside it. This means they haven't dumped the car and escaped yet. They could be on the move. The closest escape route is the Gandhinagar Railway Station. They could be headed towards the station. Perhaps they are planning to dump the car and vanish.'

It was around 11 a.m. when they suddenly spotted the i-10 across the road. Bhoopendra slammed the brakes.

'Look, there it is,' Bhoopendra said, pointing to the car parked about 70 metres away. He wanted to be sure. His pulse was racing. He took out his mobile phone and checked the license plate number of the car and then looked up to slowly verify that he had the right car. One number and alphabet at a time, taking his time as he held his breath. RJ14AC2555. Yes, this indeed was the car they were looking for. There was somebody sitting inside the car. Or was it more than one person? From this distance, he couldn't tell for sure.

He slowly turned around to look at his team. The excitement was palpable in his voice. 'That is Dushyant's car. Do not rush. I will slowly go up and see who is inside the car and ask for their ID.'

Bhoopendra then instructed the constables who were present with him. 'Suresh and Praveen, both of you stand behind the car. We don't know how many people there are in the car. If they get spooked and try to run away, both of you need to be alert to catch them. Maan and Hemant, you spread out; one ahead of the car and the other behind as a second line of defence. In case they manage to evade Suresh and Praveen. Suman, be ready to catch the woman if she is in the car. Best of luck!' Bhoopendra said as he stepped out of his vehicle. Instinctively he unclasped the holster of his service revolver. The one thing he was sure about the killers, was that they were brutal, and so he wanted to be prepared in case they were armed.

As Bhoopendra walked towards the car, he realized there were three people seated inside the car. He bent down to peer through the driver's side window. He saw a woman and two men seated like statues inside. On seeing Bhoopendra, they started behaving suspiciously. He knocked on the window that was rolled down. Immediately, the SHO slid his hand into the car and took the key out of the ignition. Now they could not drive away.

'What are your names?' Bhoopendra asked. He tried to be as calm as possible. Years of training had taught him to be alert, especially at the moment of apprehension. Aggressive criminals go into a fight or flight mode. They suddenly decide to attack the officers to eliminate them or incapacitate them. And then take flight as a last resort to escape from the inevitable. The non-aggressive ones just know there is no use of fighting and they give in. Bhoopendra had to be alert. The trio in the car seemed to be shifty. He peered in to get a better look at them.

As he kept talking, his eyes quickly scanned the interiors of the car for hidden weapons. He also quickly scanned their bodies to see if they were packing guns or weapons.

'My name is Dikshant, this is Priya and he is Lakshya,' Dikshant said, seated in the driver's seat.

'Please could you step out of the car?' Bhoopendra prompted them and lifted the lock on the driver's side from the inside and pulled the door open.

Dikshant got out. When Priya and Lakshya stepped out, they realized plainclothes police had surrounded the car.

'Yeh gaadi kahaan se mili?' (Where did you get this car from?) Bhoopendra asked.

'It belongs to a friend,' Priya said softly.

'Hmm. So where is your friend?' The question was met with silence. The three of them lowered their heads and avoided Bhoopendra's gaze.

Seeing a police inspector and a group of plainclothes police, a small crowd was beginning to gather. Suresh and Praveen stepped up to the crowd and asked,

What is it? What are you looking at? Come on, get back to your own work.'

Jo hona tha woh ho gaya . . . ab aaraam se bata do jo tumhe bolna hain.' (Whatever had to happen has happened . . . now relax and tell me what you want to say.) Bhoopendra was gentle.

Priya looked at Bhoopendra and in a matter-of-fact tone said, *'Jo aap dhund rahe ho, hum wahi hain* (We are the people who you are searching for).' Seeing a cop in uniform and a possé of cops surrounding them, Priya knew that their game was up, and yet she was defiant and proud. She wanted to have the last word, as always.

'Humara dost tha. Uske saath jhagda hua aur humne ussko murder kar diya. Galti ho gayi.' (He was our friend. We had an argument and we killed him. It was an accident.) Dikshant and Priya confided.

Lakshya piped up in a nervousness-induced tremble of a voice, *'Maine kuch nahi kiya!'* (I didn't do anything.)

'Where's the body?' Bhoopendra asked. At first, there was no reply from them. He asked again.

'We threw it on the Delhi road,' Dikshant said.

'We have found the body,' Bhoopendra informed them. This was the first time that the three of them were hearing about the police finding the body.

Having been stressed out, they had not seen the news on TV or on the mobile. This came as a shocker to them. Perhaps if they had known about the body being found, they would have made a run for it. But it was Providence that denied them the opportunity.

As an author of a book on India's serial killers, being the creator-producer-writer of *Savdhaan India* and the producer of *Crime Patrol*, I have studied crime and criminals very closely. And one of the strangest phenomena I have come across is how fate and luck play an important role in the catching of criminals.

Let us look at what could have been and how the trio could have gotten away.

They could have easily driven off on the night of the 3rd after dumping the body. But their greed got the better of them.

Dikshant did not attach the fake license plate, although he had bought it. Why did he not do it? As soon as they decided to flee the city on 4th morning, Dikshant should have changed the number plate of the car. He was too tired when he returned after dumping the body.

Remember I had told you that by falling asleep, Dikshant had made a huge mistake that would have major repercussion?

Because he slept off, he didn't change the license plate on the night of the 3rd. And he could have even changed it on the 4th morning, but he didn't. And it became the biggest giveaway that got them caught. The informant checked the number plate and reported back to the police. Checkmate!

Why use the car at all? They should've stayed at home. Why sit inside the victim's car? It is akin to sitting in the middle of a busy market soaked in blood saying, 'I killed somebody,' and drawing everyone's attention. In this case, the police. Was it necessary to use Dushyant's car? It was sheer panic. The possibility of the police coming to their doorstep had freaked them out.

Incidentally, the police would have taken at least three more days to join the dots and track them down and reach their house, or not at all. At this point, no one knew they had killed a man. It is their guilt that made them feel like they were being watched. As if the world already knew that they were the killers. In that time period they would have perhaps come to know about the discovery of the body and managed to flee. But here they were sitting in the victim's car, waiting to be picked up by the police.

As they sat in the car staring out blankly, it was as if, they had been stared down by Medusa and turned into petrified statues. It was perhaps fated that they be caught. Perhaps the Gods had tied down their feet and confounded their minds. They were too stunned to do anything. They knew they couldn't go back into the flat at Eden Garden fearing that the police could turn up at any moment. And so they sat in the car with nowhere to go, just 500 metres away from their house. And luck sided with Bhoopendra. He was able to spot the car and made it to them before they got away.

You will hear police officers often talk about 'gut feeling' and about finding things 'by chance' or by a 'stroke of luck'. This is not to take away from their hard work, perseverance and observational and investigative skills, but it's just that often things are meant to happen.

Like in 1968 when serial killer Raman Raghav literally crossed Inspector Alex Fialho on the street. The Bombay Police had been on the hunt for the dreaded serial killer and here he was walking past a policeman without panic. And when Fialho confronted him saying he has some work for him, Raghav did not try to flee or put up a fight. Instead, he just followed Fialho like a lost puppy and proceeded to sit inside the police jeep.[51] [52]

Some things are meant to happen and that is why the trio found themselves staring into the stern eyes of Gur Bhoopendra that morning.

Que Sera Sera . . .

On hearing the confession, Bhoopendra heaved a huge sigh of relief and decided to quickly shift the criminals to a secure place where a detailed interrogation would be carried out. He instructed Maan Singh and Hemant to secure Dushyant's car and get it to the Jhotwara Police Station. Bhoopendra did not want to let these three out of his sight, now that he had apprehended them. He instructed them to get into his private vehicle. The IO sat in the front. In the back seat, the lady constable sat by the window and placed Priya beside her. And Lakhsya sat on Dikshant's lap for the eleven-odd-kilometre ride.

Once they reached, the interrogation began separately. Bhoopendra first interrogated Dikshant. Then he interrogated Priya in the presence of the woman constable Suman as per law. Maan Singh interrogated Lakshya.

The interrogation was smooth and easy as the trio coughed up information easily. They confessed to the charges of kidnapping Dushyant Sharma, then murdering him, disposing of the body and also using the deceased's car to execute it all. The confession proved the IPC sections 364 A, 302, 201 imposed on them and the three were taken under arrest.

Apprehension is just Stage 1. Confession or taking the statement is Stage 2. But the most important protocol is the collection of evidence. The evidence has to match and corroborate what the criminal has confessed to and vice versa. A confession is nothing without evidence.

'Where did you commit the crime?' Bhoopendra asked.

All three of them confirmed it as '402 Eden Garden'.

Chapter Seventeen

The Evidence Collection

The confessions of Priya, Dikshant and Lakshya were recorded and documented in front of two independent witnesses. It was now time to map the scene of crime and gather the evidence.

Gur Bhoopendra, Maan Singh, the mobile forensics team, constables and the three accused headed to 402 Eden Garden, Anita Colony, Bajaj Nagar.

While you read the following pages, picture yourself standing at the crime scene as the police and the forensics team recover evidence. This is to give you, the readers, a front-seat view into the world of police investigation and evidence collection.

As Dushyant was kept captive at this flat, Section 342 of the IPC was added to the case, which is punishment for wrongful confinement. And the mobile team of the Forensic Science Laboratory (FSL) searched every corner of the apartment. Even though Dikshant and Priya had 'cleaned up' the place, there were shreds of evidences still present at the crime scene.

As soon as Bhoopendra entered the flat, he got the metallic smell of blood. And to the trained eyes of the police and the forensics team, the crime scene was brimming with evidence. The two mattresses were completely soaked in blood, so much so that the SHO could not tell what the original colour of the mattress was! He also noticed bloodstains all over the floor. He could make out that an attempt had been made to clean the floor, but in vain.

There was blood on the washbasin of the bathroom as well. The forensics team collected it through a foam strip, dried it and placed the strip inside a plastic packet and sealed. This was Exhibit C-1.

The spots of blood found on the floor of the room were also collected via foam strips, dried, sealed and marked as Exhibit C-2. There were more spots of blood found on the ply of the door. Those were collected, dried, sealed and marked as Exhibit C-3.

Dikshant had tried to wipe the blood off the floor with a mop. This was found on the floor. This became Exhibit C-4.

On the ply of the bed, a cheque was found stuck, behind which a phone number was found written: 9xxxxxxxx Ankit. As the cheque was covered with blood, it was seized as evidence and placed in a plastic packet, which was further kept in a white cloth bag, shielded and marked as Exhibit C-5.

The empty packet of Lay's chips that was covered in blood was secured as evidence and marked Exhibit C-6.

One printed cloth piece covered in blood was tagged as Exhibit C-7.

Broken pieces of a Kingfisher beer bottle found on the floor was Exhibit C-8.

The blood-splattered pair of Dushyant's Nike shoes that were found under the bed became Exhibit C-9.

A brown belt covered in blood, found near the bed was Exhibit C-10.

A coloured photocopy of Dushyant's driver's license became Exhibit C-11.

During her arrest, the lady constables had done a body/bag/cloth search on Priya and retrieved a key. It was now used to open the wooden almirah in the apartment. A mobile phone was found inside the drawer of the almirah. It was a One Plus mobile, which had two sims inside. One was a Jio number, while the other was of Vodafone, which as per Priya, belonged to Dushyant. This was marked as Exhibit-D.

The marking of evidence is done as per the location. This is to enable the proper segregation of the items, and to avoid any kind of confusion vis-à-vis the source/location at which they were recovered from, when they are used as evidence in the court of law.

The site of the body was A, the flat was C and the almirah became D.

Inside the drawer, the police also found a blood-covered Union Bank debit card that had 'Cash & Carry' printed on it. This became Exhibit D-1.

From the same drawer, Dushyant's brown wallet was recovered, inside which a debit card of Union Bank was found with the number 6069XXXXXX000XX. A Rajasthan Government Health Scheme (RGHS) card with 'health privilege' printed on it was recovered from within the wallet. A Karnataka Bank debit card bearing no. 607XXXXXXXX34XX, a Rajasthan Technical Enrolment card bearing no. 9E1JAXXXXXX12 and Dushyant's driving license bearing no RJ14/DLC/11/XXXXXX, Dushyant's PAN Card bearing number HCBXXXXXXX, his Aadhaar card were all recovered from the wallet. All of these evidence were shielded in a white cloth bag and collectively marked as Exhibit D-2.

The Rs 25,000 that Priya Seth aka Neha Seth had withdrawn the previous day from Dushyant's account was recovered and marked as Exhibit D-3.

Above that drawer in the almirah was a green-coloured zipper bag covered in blood that was torn from one side. Inside the torn bag was a floral printed wallpaper, one printed bed sheet of white, green and red colour covered in blood, an old used scarf covered in blood and one black cable wire covered in blood having 2 separate knots on it were recovered, shielded in a white cloth bag, marked as Exhibit D-4.

Dikshant and Priya who had cleared up the room kept staring as the cops scanned every inch of the apartment and pulled out evidence from every nook and corner.

'Sir, we have recovered this ladies' sandal from the almirah,' said one of the constables.

Gur Bhoopendra noted that the pair belonged to the Mochi brand.

'Turn it around,' Bhoopendra instructed the constable, who turned the pair of sandals around to expose the soles to his boss. The soles of the sandals had dried blood on them. Bhoopendra visualized the floor of the room covered in blood, with the victim lying on the floor inside the trolley bag as Priya walked across the room in her Mochi sandals, leaving bloody prints on the floor.

'That's evidence. Secure it,' he instructed. The sandals were packed and marked as Exhibit D-5.

The pair of almirah keys that Priya had used to open the almirah were recovered as evidence and placed in a white cloth bag, shielded and marked as D-6.

'Where is the knife that you used to stab Dushyant?' Bhoopendra asked Priya and Dikshant. The latter pointed to a wooden almirah in the corner of the hall.

'Where are the keys?' the IO asked and one of the constables produced it. The set of keys had been taken off Dikshant through body/clothes search at the time of his arrest.

Bhoopendra opened the almirah and pulled out one of the drawers. Bingo! Inside was the bloodstained knife. As per the Seizure Panchnama, every piece of evidence collected had to be described in detail so that there is no discrepancy later. Therefore, the knife handle was measured as 5 inches long and the blade was measured to be 7 inches long, with the word ICE printed on the handle of the knife. The murder weapon is always the most crucial piece of evidence as it inadvertently has the fingerprints of the killer (unless they are wearing gloves), and also the DNA of the victim, thus becoming the 'one' piece of evidence that connects the dots and binds the killer to the victim and the crime. The knife was wrapped in a paper and shielded in a white cloth bag, marked as Exhibit-E.

'E' because it was a new source from which evidence was lifted.

An old grey-coloured pair of jeans covered in blood was also pulled out of the same almirah and marked as Exhibit E-1

A plastic carry bag with the word 'Safari' printed on it that was also soaked in blood was marked as Exhibit E-2.

The almirah keys recovered from the accused Dikshant was also shielded in a white cloth bag and marked as exhibit E-3.

The recovery place was mapped and documented. The FSL mobile unit present on the spot then took pictures of the crime spot. The original rent agreement of the flat between Priya and the owner Mrs Neelam Yadav was produced and included in the documents.

As per process, all ten of Dikshant's fingernails were clipped by a nail cutter, wrapped in a white paper and marked as Exhibit F-1. It joined the plethora of evidence that had been collected.

Priya's fingernails were similarly collected and marked as Exhibit F-2.

And Lakshya's clipped fingernails were secured and marked as Exhibit F-3.

Why did the police clip and collect their fingernails?

During a physical assault, biological evidence may be transferred between the victim and assailant. For instance, if the victim scratches the assailant, skin cells can be trapped beneath fingernails and vice versa. Thus nail evidence is regularly collected by the forensics team and sent to the crime laboratory

The old Nike shoes that Dushyant had worn was collected as evidence and marked as Exhibit-G.

So if he had been wearing socks and they would have been collected as evidence, then what is the Exhibit number that would be assigned to it?

Exhibit-G1! Well done!

If Lakshya thought that his flat would not be searched, he was wrong. Bhoopendra and his team now headed to Lakshya's house at 402, second floor, Tanishq Apartment, Malviya Nagar, Jaipur.

At his flat, a blood-soaked pair of jeans and shirt were recovered from under the mattress. It was marked as Exhibit I. A blood-soaked handkerchief was found inside the pocket of the jeans and marked as Exhibit I–1. The blood-soaked shirt was seized as evidence and marked as exhibit I–2.

Now it was time to take a look at the car and tie it comprehensively to the case, so as to prove that the killers had indeed carried Dushyant's body in the car.

In the eyes of the Indian judiciary, the accused is innocent until proven guilty. Even though the accused may have made confessions or given signed statements, it becomes the duty and the prerogative of the police or the State to gather all evidence and prove that the accused is guilty via trial in court. So collecting evidence is of prime importance so as to build a watertight case against the accused.

The officer of the FSL mobile unit (Jaipur) went to the Jhotwara Police Station to examine and document the Hyundai i-10 car RJ14AC2555 as evidence. Visible inspection of the car was done followed by clicking of pictures of the car.

According to the prosecution's lawyer, Sandeep Luhadia, 'more than 100 articles were recovered'.[53]

Bhoopendra requested the phone service providers to help out with the Call Data Records (CDR) of Dikshant's two phone numbers: 7500XXXXX7 and 9413XXXXX5, Lakshya's two numbers: 9928XXXXX2 and 7014XXXXX6, and Priya's number 8740XXXXX9. The police also extracted the CDR of Dushyant's two numbers and his father Rameshwar's.

As per the procedure guidelines, the post-mortem report of Dushyant along with three jars of viscera collected from the body by the medical board was taken from pathology of Kanwatia Hospital, Jaipur, and were documented.

Dushyant's Union Bank account records were extracted and documented.

The three of them were once again taken back to Jhotwara Police Station and interrogated separately. And they spilled the beans without much persuasion.

Bhoopendra and his team had secured one part of the crime, which was the actual scene of crime. Now the peripherals needed to be secured. He now concentrated on the disposal of the body.

This interrogation revealed details about:

1. The trolley bags that they had purchased from Sodala
2. The fake license plate
3. The filling up of petrol at Jhalana

And so another round of chasing the evidence took place.

This round of questioning revealed that when the trio were on their way to dispose of the body, they noticed that Dushyant's car was running low on fuel. So they stopped at the petrol pump at Jhalana to fill petrol.

* * *

Constable Battu was sent off to the petrol station to Shaheed Bastiram Petrol Pump at Jhalana, which is approximately 14 kilometres away from the Jhotwara Police Station to see if there was a possibility of getting the CCTV footage of the murderers arriving, filling petrol and exiting.

Seeing a constable arrive on the premises spooked some of the attendants who began to whisper and wonder.

'*Manager kahan hai?*' (Where is the manager?) Battu asked one of the attendants who was rolling a tyre on the floor after having repaired a puncture. The man pointed towards the office area of the filling station. Battu walked towards the building. Having seen a constable arrive on the CCTV monitor, the manager stepped out.

'Are you the manager?' Battu asked.

'Yes. Myself Prakash Chand Sain, the Manager.'

'Good, we need to talk.' Saying this he gently nudged Prakash towards the same office building that he had stepped out of, and the duo walked inside and disappeared. The attendants who had been staring at the proceedings got back to work, as if their hypnosis had just suddenly worn off.

Constable Battu explained and divulged as little information as he could but communicated the urgency and the importance of acquiring the CCTV of the 3rd Prakash did not want the police to be hanging around at the filling station as it was bad for business. So he promptly transferred the footage on a 8 GB HP pen drive. This was marked as Exhibit-M. The information given by the petrol pump manager was documented. He also gave a certificate under Section 65B of the Evidence Act that was included.

65B deals with 'conditions for the admissibility of electronic evidence.' It states: 'If any information contained in an electronic record that is printed in paper, stored, recorded, or copied in optical or magnetic media, produced by a computer, shall be deemed as a document.'

And so the CCTV footage of the filling station was officially a document of evidence.

Under the Indian Evidence Act, 1872, Section 65B prescribes a distinct framework that governs the admissibility of electronic evidence. There have been multiple litigations over the scope and ambit of Section 65B.

For legal-eagles who want to know more about 65B of the Evidence Act, I am including a footnote for you to read up on.[54]

* * *

'And then what did you do?' Bhoopendra prodded.

'We bought a fake number plate so that we could continue to use Dushyant's car and drive it around and escape in it,' Dikshant mumbled.

'Did you give the shop your ID as per law?'

Dikshant nodded, 'Yes, sir. I gave my Aadhaar card.'

This was good news. Another evidence that tied the trio to the crime, to the disposal of the body and further criminal intent to continue using the victim's car.

Bhoopendra and a constable accompanied Dikshant to the shop. Seeing the police descend upon his shop, the owner almost shat his pants.

'What is your name?'

'Sirji, Suryaprakash,' the owner replied shakily.

'Iss aadmi ko pehechantay ho?' (Do you know this person?) the cop asked.

Suryaprakash had no clue that the vehicle number Dikshant had given was a fake one. So Suryaprakash confidently replied in the affirmative.

'Sir, issko maine number plate becha tha.' (Sir, I had sold him a number plate.)

'Gaadi ke papers verify kiye bina? Gaadi ka number fake tha!' (Without doing a proper verification of the vehicle documents? The number given was a fake one!) The cop blasted the owner.

Suryaprakash immediately knew he was in trouble. The cop showed him the number plate with RJ14AQ4384, 'This is it, right?'

Suryaprakash just nodded, not knowing what fate awaited him.

'What ID card did he give you?' It was time to get down to collecting the evidence.

'Sir, Aadhaar card.'

'Show me.'

After searching through a few drawers and files, Suryaprakash came back with a photocopy of Dikshant's Aadhaar card. The police seized the photocopy and marked it as evidence and Suryaprakash's statement was documented.

Here Dikshant could have easily given Dushyant's Aadhaar card instead of his own to Suryaprakash when he was purchasing the license plate and that would have meant one less piece of incriminating evidence that tied him to the crime and intent.

* * *

The third piece of the puzzle was the Koralite trolley bags that they had purchased.

Bhoopendra, Hemant, Priya, Dikshant and Constable Suman headed to Sodala. There, the duo identified the shop. The shop owner Kamal Meghani was interrogated, and he confirmed that he had sold two such trolley bags to the duo.

Next on the cards was the site of the kidnapping. Although it was not a 'kidnapping' in the traditional sense, where the victim was forcibly picked up and abducted. It was the location where the kidnapper and the victim met, and the moment marked the beginning of the modus operandi—the kidnapping. So that location became the de facto kidnapping site.

Bhoopendra and Constable Suman accompanied Priya in the police jeep. Priya pointed out the kidnapping spot at Bhaskar Pulia or Bhaskar Bridge.

'I called him two or three times and directed him to come here. When he came, I got into his car and then gave directions to my flat,' Priya mumbled to the police. The place was mapped and documented after a visible inspection and confirmation by Priya.

The sub inspectors and the constables also met the two watchmen who worked at Eden Garden: Bhagwan and Shyam Sundar Sharma, and took their statements. They confirmed seeing a man drive an i-10 car and arrive with Priya on the evening of the 2nd. They also confirmed seeing Dikshant park the car next to the lift, to which they had objected. At that point, Priya and Dikshant had backed their argument saying the trolley bag was heavy and that's why they had parked the car next to the lift. The watchmen then saw the trolley bag being loaded into the car, and the duo driving off.

The three criminals were taken next to Kanwatia Hospital and blood samples were taken for DNA tests. In total, twenty-five liquids were sent for examination to Vidhi Vigyan Laboratory, Jaipur.

'Seth seemed convinced that she would get bail, just like she had got it in her previous crimes,' said one of the officers.

On 4 May, when reporters descended upon Jhotwara Police Station to interview the accused and the police officers, Priya screamed in defiance, 'Is this the first murder committed in India?' The press was shocked.

When the news broke about the killers being apprehended, their faces were flashed all across tv channels, and newspapers not just in Rajasthan but across India.

IO (Investigating Officer) Nidhi had also been keeping up with the case as one is wont to do being a cop. The discovery of the packed body had earlier sent a shockwave through the police community of Rajasthan. And Nidhi also came to know about the arrest of the three people behind the crime. But it was not until she saw Priya's face on TV that her jaw dropped in shock.

She immediately recalled the cheating case that had been lodged against her in Vaishali Nagar by Gurujar Singh, and where Nidhi had been posted.

'She looked so innocent then . . . I can't believe she is capable of doing something so heinous,' Nidhi recalled when I met her.

Bhoopendra instructed his team to reach out to the families of the three.

Dikshant's academician father was completely shocked. He just couldn't fathom how his son had become a murderer!

Lakshya's mom was devastated. 'I am a single mom and with great difficulty I had sent him to study here in Jaipur. I am educating my daughter also. Now, with him behind bars, how will I run the house?'

Priya's parents had cut off all relationship with her since she started getting arrested, and running her escort business. It was only her sister who had kept in touch. But the family could not see how a studious girl like Priya was capable of taking someone else's life!

The investigation joined the dots on the phone number 8740988XXX registered under the name of Om Prakash, which had popped up in Dushyant's call records of the evening of 2nd. There had been three short calls and the phone had been switched off earlier. When the police followed the trail of the number, it was revealed that Priya was using this sim registered under the name of Om Prakash. When she was asked how she got hold of the sim, she did not have any conclusive answer. It turns out the sim originated at Jai Mata Di Sim Shop at Bhankrota. The owner, Deepak Kumar, had sold it to Om Prakash. Then, the sim was stolen from Om Prakash. Then it was bundled together with other stolen sims and sold off at a throwaway price *ala* the Jamtara Model. Om Prakash had, in fact, registered a complaint when his sim was stolen. And Priya used one number for each of her cons, so that the victim wouldn't be able to reach her or track her, once the con had been executed.

Shailabh Rawat, editor of the true crime publications *Madhur Kathayein* and *Mahanagar Kahaniyan*, says, 'The Internet allows for a wide range of deception. Crimes such as blackmail and honey trapping have been made much easier by social media. Honey trapping is a hot trend. It is low-investment. All men have a weakness for women. If you lay a trap for ten, one will fall for it.'[55]

A board of doctors conducted the post-mortem procedure that included Dr Ajay Srivastava, Dr Nasreen Bharti, Dr Himmat Singh and Dr Suresh Kumar Bhaskar. Dr Bhaskar confirmed the post-mortem procedure stating that there were a total of eleven injuries found on Dushyant. On examination, hematoma[56] was found in the neck muscle on both sides and the laryngeal cavity, tracheal cavity and bronchus. Swelling was found above the nose and a fracture of the nose was found. All injuries were ante-mortem (before death) and the cause of death was found to be asphyxia[57] due to body injuries.

Priya had ruined the lives of hundreds, maybe thousands, of people through her cons, but now her new identity was that of a cold-blooded murderer. And things were about to get worse.

Chapter Eighteen

The Interview That Shocked the World

Deepika Narayan Bhardwaj is an Indian journalist, documentary film-maker and men's rights activist. Deepika rose to prominence after producing the documentary *Martyrs of Marriage*, which covered the abuse of criminal section 498A (anti-dowry law) by brides and their families to entrap men with false charges.

It was her video interview[58] with the three accused that went viral on YouTube and people across the world met the cold-blooded, I care-a-damn, psychopath Priya Seth for the first time on 25 June 2008, i.e., fifty-two days after the trio had been arrested. Suddenly, the Jaipur Tinder case became a huge rage thanks to the media. It was also a favourite whipping horse for news channels as they projected the case to be the fallout of social media and made Tinder sound like a place where people of loose morals congregated in the hope of a hook-up. The perception was those looking for real relationships and love had migrated to Bumble and Hinge. So the media was partially right, but then again generalizations are prone to be also tinged with dollops of bias and agendas.

Needless to say, this was a great opportunity for the media to take a stab at the 'online/virtual' world—a nemesis that both of them had been at loggerheads with as the online world married with ever-improving technology made the print and television rather redundant.

Needless to say, one of the first things that struck the people at court when the trio were brought in for their remand hearing was Priya's attitude. Although her face did not betray her inner thoughts and emotions, she held her head up and walked with confidence in her designer shoes. Her gait and demeanour were devoid of any remorse.

Deepika, who had always been interested in women who abuse the loopholes and gender biases in the Indian law to get away, especially when it comes to women committing crimes against men, found this case interesting. And she promptly got special permission as a journalist to interview the trio, the IO and Dushyant's father Rameshwar.

The interview footage that emerged in 2018 sent chills down the spines of the viewers as Priya displayed her entitlement, pushing her own fabricated story of innocence and justification, blind to the heinous crime she had just orchestrated.

At this point in time, in 2018, I had no intention of writing this book—I was just aghast at Priya and her matter-of-fact interview.

It was much later in 2022, by the time I had two true-crime bestsellers and I had been studying criminal behaviour closely and writing about it for *Savdhaan India* and *Crime Patrol*, that the idea came to write this book—as an all-access look at the crime and the criminals. And I must thank Deepika Narayan Bhardwaj for giving the world the first glimpse of the trio.

I studied the video interview once again minute by minute, second by second—this time by going into the heads of the three criminals to study their thoughts, their body language, their motives and the language they used to convey their thoughts. What you are about to read will take you deep into their heads . . .

The interview clip begins with Priya casually flicking her hair back over her left shoulder. All the while she smiles and says, 'These days, when I see a camera, I feel like breaking it.' Her smile is natural and she looks away from the camera, as if we have caught a celebrity mid-conversation at a party and she is making a casual statement about the paparazzi harassing her.

Now from here on, there are three versions to *who took the decision to kill Dushyant?* And *who carried out the murder?*

1. Priya's version: the planning is done by her and Dikshant, but the act of the murder is done wholly and solely by Dikshant, aided partially by Lakshya. She is a mere spectator.
2. Dikshant's version: This puts Priya in the dock for planning and also nails her as the murderer.
3. Lakshya's version: In this version, Priya and Dikshant are co-conspirators, while Lakshya is the spectator.

Priya's version

'Dushyant' as she says his name, her body language and facial expression break down for a second before she regains her composure. It is a momentary lapse of poise and confidence, which perhaps is reflective of a fleeting sense of regret, before she lapses back into the Priya Seth.

'I did not even know Dushyant's name. I met him on Tinder. He did not even tell me his real name, real identity. He told me he was very rich, has lots of money . . .'

There is a long sigh here before she continues. And all the while, she does not look directly into the camera, even once. Her head and eyes dart all around the room.

During police interrogation, one of the primary things that the interrogator looks out for to study non-verbal human behaviour, is to look for breaks in eye contact. The eyes are the most expressive area and they communicate without using words. It is the window to our soul and thoughts.

Losing eye contact during the response is commonly interpreted as deceitful behavior. The break in eye contact is where the subject is mentally running away from you.

Many inexperienced interrogators often make the mistake of challenging the subject to look them in the eye while responding to the questions. This is a huge no-no! As this creates 'false eye contact', when the suspect is forced to look at the cop, and the interrogator loses the advantage of being able to read the true and real breaks in eye contact that may or may not lead to clues or a lead.

If 'false eye contact' happens, then the interrogator must fall back on studying the body language of the accused as usually, the breaks in eye contact are accompanied by other deceptive body language cues—ticks, a monotonous action like scratching, restless shaking of the legs, quick batting of the eyelids are often signs of nervousness.

'I was living in with Dikshant and he had a debt of Rs 21 lakh.'

And this is where we get a glimpse into her mind. Her micro-expressions of constantly blinking and a sudden jerk to her head to look down before uttering the following sentence is interesting, as she pins the 'need' for the crime on Dikshant.

'He was looking for someone to get that money from.'

And it is here that Priya, knowingly or unknowingly, legally defines the motive for the crime, and that the motive came from Dikshant Kamra. It was *he* who was looking for someone, it wasn't *we*.

I love legalese and getting under the legal skin to dissect it and see what interpretations it has . . . And so let's study about 'motive'.

Whenever a crime is committed, the court always takes into account the offender's motive for committing the crime and the preparation made in committing the crime. There is always a motive behind every act.

According to Advocate Sanjeev Sirohi, 'It is motive that propels and acts as a catalyst responsible for any act being committed. Therefore, its importance in analysing the real reason behind any offender committing any crime can hardly be overstated. Many difficult cases have been solved by the courts by evaluating motive and correlating it with the facts and circumstances of those cases.'

And he goes on to cite the case of *Shreekantiah Ramayya Munipalli v. The State of Bombay*, 1955, where the Supreme Court rightly observed: 'It has to be kept in mind that a person does not commit a grave illegal act which might expose him to prosecution and possible disgrace unless he is prompted by some strong motive.'[59]

And Priya had pinned the 'motive' squarely on Dikshant and his debts.

In the video, she goes on to say, 'So we made this plan together that we will kidnap someone, ask for ransom and then kill that person. We had planned the murder already. It wasn't fixed who it would be, when it would be but it was planned.'

And here in the video, it is perhaps her hubris that makes her confess to having made the plans and intention to murder even before the kidnapping. Did she think of herself as a star being interviewed and getting media attention? So much so that she let her guard down, let her street-smart instincts disappear and casually admit that it was a pre-planned murder, not realizing that this video could become her nemesis and admission of guilt? There would be no way the court could overlook this video.

In a criminal case, the motive and the intent are two foundations on which the case is built upon. And next are the modus operandi, the act, the nature and the extent of the crime. Priya already established the motive and intent.

'So when I met Dushyant and he lied that he is very rich, we kidnapped him and asked for ransom. But later we realized he didn't have anything.'

At this point, journalist Deepika Bhardwaj poses the question to Priya:

'Dushyant's father gave you money. But you still killed him (Dushyant). Why?'

And this is the first WTF moment in the video when Priya looks dead straight at the camera, and in one remorseless hurried breath, she casually says, 'We killed him before we got the money!' And then she continues to stare expressionless at the camera. There are no micro-expressions, no batting of eyelids, nothing! Then the video dissolves into the next question. Her cavalier attitude is what shook the world. She didn't have an iota of guilt or remorse. It was as if she was sure of this one thing, of this one decision—so much so that she could look straight at you and declare it without hesitation. While she kept looking away as she 'cooked' the story, here she knew exactly what she was saying! Shocking and blood-curdling!!

Deepika: 'How did you kill him?'

And here is the second masterstroke by Priya. She projects herself as an observer who merely 'watched' rather than physically 'commits' the act of crime. A few sentences ago she had confessed to making the plans with Dikshant. But so cleverly she makes a distinction to separate the act of planning and preparation for a crime, and the actual act of committing the crime.

She dons the garb of Lady Macbeth.

In William Shakespeare's eponymous play, Macbeth declares that he no longer intends to kill Duncan. Lady Macbeth outraged, calls him a coward and questions his manhood: 'When you durst do it,' she says, 'then you were a man' (1.7.49). He asks her what will happen if they fail; she promises that as long as they are bold, they will be successful. Then she tells him her plan.

Uncannily Priya appears to be Lady Macbeth to Dikshant's Macbeth and Dushyant's Duncan. Priya makes the plan and then as per her version, gets Dikshant to kill, much like in Macbeth.

And here is how Priya pinned the act of the murder on Dikshant. 'First Dikshant strangled him. He survived.

Then Lakshya smothered him with a pillow. He became unconscious but still didn't die. Dikshant then asked me to get him a knife and slit his throat. He died.' So according to Priya, it is Dikshant who, aided by Lakshya, tries to kill Dushyant and then it is Dikshant who asks her to get the murder weapon. She transforms herself from being the mastermind to the reluctant accomplice, being manipulated by Dikshant!

It is very difficult to believe anything that Priya says, considering her criminal past, the natural talent of weaving yarns and the propensity to hoodwink people, without remorse and for the sake of her selfish benefit. And of course her version has massive holes. And her smart-ass answers reveal more than she would like to.

- She implicates Lakshya as smothering Dushyant. This is an attempt on her part to take Lakshya down with her and Dikshant. The truth is Lakshya handed the pillow over to Dikshant.
- She says Dikshant asked her to get a knife, which she got for him. This is another spin. Priya was the one who went out to get the knife from the kitchen.

What Deepika's video does next, is to reveal Priya's past and this is the next WTF moment that shows you her callous, dispassionate and psychotic avatar, and reveals the story about the knife.

As soon as Deepika starts to ask the question, you see her eyes narrow and anger creep into her eyes because she knows where this question is headed and she doesn't like it. It is because her past intentions connect to the present murder. It is the glimpse into her ruthless, entitled mind.

Deepika: The investigation officer of an earlier case says you told her that you got the knife to kill your ex-boyfriend . . .

The ex-boyfriend that Deepika was referring to was Gurujar Singh whom she had blackmailed in 2017–18. Before Deepika can finish asking her the question, Priya interjects with a breathless tirade.

Priya: No. I didn't buy that knife to kill him. My ex-boyfriend is a liar of the first order and a sick man. He filed a false case on me. It would be good if he dies. *(And this is where Priya in her excitement reveals)* I actually had to murder him only, but I didn't do it.

And here she looks up and laughs. The act of murder, the power to snuff out someone's life is reduced to a callous joke, a matter-of-fact statement. And she confesses in her trademark cavalier manner that she should have murdered him when she had the chance to. But she perhaps realizes that she has screwed up and revealed something she should not have and changes the story . . .

Priya: I brought (sic) that knife to cut my own nerve (sic) and actually did it.

And she sits back rolling her eyes, and batting her eyelids furiously, looking like a sulking, malfunctioning robot.

The fact that she had thought about killing somebody and had even procured a probable weapon really helps us to understand her mind. Her spoilt-brat tantrums of her childhood of always getting what she wants had transformed her into psychotic monster.

Her decision to kill Gurujar was due to her not getting her own way. Her plan of blackmailing had flopped. And now instead of throwing a tantrum, she was willing to murder. In her head, the tantrum had upped the stakes.

Similarly, the decision to kill Dushyant stemmed from the fact that firstly, she had been outwitted and out-bluffed. And secondly she was not getting what she had planned for. The decision was mainly driven by her Id: the stubborn subconscious that was not willing to accept defeat.

Do you remember kids from your childhood, the ones in the locality who owned the cricketing gear and when dismissed would throw a tantrum and walk away mid-game with the wickets and the cricket bat? Now multiply that tantrum to a hundred and here Priya had to spend a week in jail as Gurujar had called her bluff and had gotten her arrested! And boy, was she still pissed at him!

Her breathless tirade comes to an end and her expression is that of anger. Deepika allows the scene to continue instead of cutting away. Priya sits back and her expression softens as for the first time we get to see a sense of frustration in her with the realization that it is all over. Deepika asks her if she had stabbed Dushyant? This time, a much softer Priya says no, she didn't.

And the biggest lie in her statement is 'Dikshant slit his throat.' When ten stab wounds were found on Dushyant's neck, why didn't she say 'stabbed'? The action of stabbing is very clearly different from slitting the throat. And she was a smart, educated girl who would know the difference. So was this the wrong ingredient in the soup of lies she was cooking to implicate Dikshant solely via the video interview?

Her version is replete with contradictions and holes. Deepika would go on to interview the other two, and not surprisingly they tried to implicate each other, and minimize their own participation in the crime. So here is Version 2 of what happened seen through the eyes of Dikshant Kamra.

Dikshant's version

He seems more relaxed. But he too exhibits the same chilling matter-of-fact demeanour as he narrates his side of the story.

Dikshant: 'I met Priya through Tinder app. We spoke and met the next day. We started speaking on the phone and got emotionally attached. She took a flat and I shifted with her. I was about to start my YouTube channel, as I was free for three months. We became closer. Priya lied to me that she works in a travel agency called Vasu Holidays and I trusted her. Later I got to know about her reality, but I couldn't find a way to leave her and escape. During Dushyant's murder fiasco, I wasn't aware of anything. At the last moment, she told me about the murder plan. Lakshya has also agreed with me on this . . .

The subtitle here is a little dodgy. What Kamra actually means is that Lakshya agreed to do the kidnapping and torture (the subtitles make it look like Lakshya agreed to the murder OR the fact that Priya told them about the murder plan at the last minute and Lakshya is proof to that statement).

Dikshant: 'Earlier she said we will just torture him, ask for ransom and leave the next day and we agreed to do it. We then tortured him and we have confessed to it in our statement. But it is Priya who murdered him. It was all her plan. First attack of knife was also by her. Till the end it is she who stabbed him. This is my statement and I stand by it.'

Like the classic aftermath of criminals getting caught, they tried to slap the blame on the mastermind or the one who looks the most probable amongst them. Here it is Priya; she had manipulated both Dikshant and Lakshya. So the boys could be telling the truth. After all, Priya had the acumen and the skill to come up with the plan, had that streak of violence in her and could manipulate people. Or was Dikshant regretting his decision of carrying out the task on Priya's bidding?

And here is Version 3 of what happened according to Lakshya Walia.

Lakshya's version

Lakshya, who found himself at the wrong place, at the wrong time, among wrong company had a mathematical version. When Deepa asks him who planned the murder, Lakshya replies: 'Well 70 per cent Priya's and 30 per cent Dikshant's.' And he immediately contradicts it.

Lakshya: 'Murder was entirely Priya's plan. She earlier told Dikshant that we will threaten him, scare him and then leave him. In the morning she said we will have to kill him or all three of us will be caught.'

Is Lakshya attributing 30 per cent blame on Dikshant because of his friend's betrayal and getting him embroiled in this case? After all, Lakshya had been a good friend and allowed Dikshant to stay with him when the latter had turned up from Mumbai with trouble on his heels. Maybe, this was his way of telling Dikshant, 'Screw You!'

And how does one quantify blame? Thirty per cent sounds like pass marks for an exam! But Lakshya's statement clearly makes Priya the mastermind.

Once the statements are done, the video interview goes into Priya's modus operandi and how she used to con men. One of the newspaper clippings in the video has the headline of 'Over the past 8 years Priya has conned 1000 men!'

Priya: 'I used to defraud people through an escort website that I used to run. I ran the service but did not provide girls. I used to take money from the client and run away . . .'

At this point a mischievous smile plays on her lips, like an impish schoolgirl who had placed the worm on the teacher's desk, much to the delight of the other kids in the classroom. She tries to control the laugh as the joke perhaps plays out in her head as she recalls the thousands of men that she has managed to hoodwink.

Priya: 'Without providing him any girl as an escort.'

Deepika: 'Run away with money as in?'

Priya: 'As in if someone asked for a call girl, I used to go and meet the client myself and take money from him. Then I used to make an excuse that I need to pay the driver and run away from there with money. That's it.'

Deepika: 'How many men you've done this with?'

Priya: 'More than a thousand men.'

Deepika: 'How long were you doing this?'

Priya: 'About six or seven years.'

Deepika: 'No one ever complained?'

Priya: 'No.'

As we know, Priya's modus operandi was pretty watertight. She worked on two conditions: she always targeted people who were married or 'looked' married (older men who were looking for sex with younger women). And she chose people who were from outside Jaipur. The first condition made sure the men would not lodge complaints with the police, as that would expose their escapade. And the latter ensured they would not know where to go to lodge the complaint. And also it dissuaded them as lodging a complaint would mean that the complainant would need to travel to

Jaipur every time the investigation was on, or there was a court date.

Deepika, at this point in the video, asks about the infamous incident of Priya heading off to con another man straight after the murder. One can see Priya's eyes narrow down and she corrects Deepika.

Priya: 'Yes, I went. But I did not have the body with me at that time. We had thrown the body by then. I went later in the evening. The body was dumped in the afternoon.'

She talks matter-of-factly, without showing any signs of emotion or anger. She just wants to ensure the facts are correct. Deepika realizes that Priya has completely missed the incredulity of the situation and decides to ask her the same question but with a slightly more 'sensational' line of questioning.

Deepika: 'So you went to extort someone even after the murder?'

As soon as Priya hears the question, it has the desired effect as she springs to not only defend herself but also shock us with what she says. In an aggressive, cocky and self-assured tone, her nostrils flared in anger, Priya admonishes Deepika, 'This isn't called extortion, madam. You better check the definition of extortion on the Internet first. They ask for a call girl first and pay money for that. How can you call that extortion? Define extortion please. I did not blackmail them.'

Priya is technically right. Deepika used the wrong word. Instead of conning, she used extortion. But it got the reaction she was looking for. And Priya by this time is fuming, and she looks away from the camera.

Deepika's voice softens as she asks, 'So you used to offer a service, did not provide it but take (sic) money for it?'

And this is the mother-of-all WTF moments in the video. When I watched it in 2018, it was something that really shook me and the rest of the world too. We got to dive right into the warped, depraved and psychotic mind of Priya Seth.

Priya sneers and replies, 'These men used to leave their wives at home and contact us for getting a girl . . . I don't want to use bad words . . . we used to take money from them but did not provide any girl. I think I used to serve such people right by doing so. In fact I was doing social service, which has stopped now!'

In her twisted, depraved, psychotic mind, she justified the conning of the men as service to the society, as she taught these men a lesson to not stray from their marriages! This moment in the video truly defined Priya's mind. The world got to see how she had concocted this story in her head and justified the crimes that she was committing.

The video ends with Rameshwar being interviewed. Dushyant's photograph can be seen behind him.

Rameshwar: 'I have lost my son but if these people are released on bail anyhow, they would do it to someone else. My request is to highlight this case so much that these people get death penalty. Only then I will be at peace.'

The accused were examined under Section 313 the Penal Procedure Code. And not surprisingly, Lakshya claimed to have been framed. He claimed he neither drank alcohol nor had ganja. He even claimed that he never went to Eden Garden Flat No. 402 to either drink, or be part of the kidnapping scheme, or asking for ransom. He accused the police team of planting evidence to frame him. He said he did not travel by car with Dikshant or with Priya, did not visit the petrol pump, nor did he help in disposing of the body.

Priya too feigned innocence stating she too was falsely implicated and that she does not know who Lakshya Walia and Dikshant Kamra are as she had never met them previously. And her lover Dikshant too pleaded innocence saying he was being framed.

Were these three stupid? They had just confessed their crime on video and yet here they were claiming innocence and stating that they were being framed.

To get the guilty behind bars, the police not only have to collect the evidence but also arrange it in the correct sequence and logic, along with the lawyer's arguments and try to connect and bind the evidence to the criminals. This is done to avoid the criminals from getting away citing the argument of 'circumstantial evidence'.

And Gur Bhoopendra Singh knew that although he had custody of the accused, and that there was a video interview, the real test would come in the court of law.

Chapter Nineteen

The Diva

It was 12 September 2018. There was a palpable current running through the Jaipur Sessions Court. The 'Tinder Killers'—term coined by the press—were to make their first appearance in court. The crowd of journalists edged each other to root themselves at vantage points from where they could see the killers alight from the police van and enter the courthouse premises.

Over the past four months, Jaipur and the rest of the country had been shocked, stunned by the unfolding of the murder mystery. Plus, everyone had voyeuristically consumed every bit of information that appeared in the news with regard to the Tinder Killer trio. And with each lurid detail, the image of the killers, especially Priya Seth became a point of conversation. There was great interest to find out what she smoked, drank, wore, spent; her monthly expenses, her favourite perfume, her sense of dressing, her ability to lure men, and the apparent crores that she had earned by deceiving them.

The news reports came in thick and fast, as she had become a household name in the Pink City. She smoked Marlboro and drank Black Label whisky. A report even stated that she drank the Himalayan brand of mineral water. *Dainik Bhaskar* said that her branded shoes from Mumbai cost Rs 35,000. Another report from the same newspaper quoted the shoes to be worth Rs 80,000 and her designer watch Rs 45,000. Her haul was estimated to be worth Rs 1.75 crore. The newspaper also calculated her monthly expense to be Rs 2 lakh. Meanwhile *Rajasthan Patrika* was quoted saying she liked 'expensive perfumes, clothes, cosmetics and air travel' and it also calculated her monthly expenses to be 'Rs 1.5 lakh'.[60]

Priya Seth did not give up on her luxury lifestyle. 'She asked her lawyer to appeal to the court to allow her to smoke in jail. Can you believe that!' exclaimed Sandeep Luhadia, prosecution's lawyer, and he also mentioned that her shoes were worth Rs 75,000.[61]

What's with the journalists and the lawyers obsessing over her shoes?

Journalist Snigdha Poonam writes in her article 'Lady Killers' for *Open* magazine:

> The three of them hired separate lawyers and threw the blame at one another. Seth, however, became the face of the killing—a female criminal of the kind that hits the news cycle once or twice in a generation . . . Everyone I met in Jaipur had a theory about her. A local journalist also covering the case told me her actions had a simple explanation: no woman born so beautiful would be

content with a regular life. Her lawyer also believed she wasn't cut out for simple living. He believed she was too smart for that. 'That girl, she can make a fool out of any man,' he said, summing up her deceptive talents as 'an art.' When you have a mind like that, he said, money chases you and not you, it . . . .[62]

When the trio of Priya Seth, her lover Dikshant Kamra and his erstwhile classmate Lakshya Walia entered the court premises, everybody wanted to get a dekko of the cold-blooded killers.

Poonam recalls their first court appearance in an article she wrote for the *Hindustan Times*, where she described Priya as 'small and slight, she was dressed in a yellow kurta, black salwar, and a golden dupatta'.[63] Her face was paler than the police mug shots, with dark circles around her eyes, and her straight, brown hair shorter. Priya was the centre of attraction that day. No one even noticed the two boys walking behind her. Priya became quite the star since the video interview had gone viral. Or maybe the Jaipur Police believed in ladies first.

Dikshant, in an orange shirt and black jeans, wore a smirk on his face along with his styled beard. And Lakshya followed him wearing a blue shirt, black joggers and a downturned scowl. But nobody looked at the boys.

The people nudged each other, whispering their comments and observations looking at Priya. She looked fragile, and the crowd probably expected her to break down. After all, the two boys had implicated her to be the mastermind behind the murder. But as she took the stand, she seemed nonchalant about what was going on. Her face was plain, sans any expression—just like her remorseless interview.

But everybody knew that behind that deadpan expression lay one of the most cold-blooded murderers of the country.

Shailabh Rawat, who is the editor of *Madhur Kathayein* and *Mahanagar Kahaniyan* since 1986, spoke to Poonam of *Hindustan Times* about the Priya Seth case:

> Priya Seth's case is different from that of the average female criminal. Often, they transition from being victims to perpetrators in revenge or rebellion, for example Delhi's flesh trade don Sonu Punjaban who was pushed into a life of crime through a series of relationships with criminals. Also, most female criminals are only noted for one case. Seth was never a victim. She is also a serial or professional criminal from what we know. Whatever she allegedly did—blackmail, honey trap or murder—she did at her own behest. She breaks all the rules.[64]

During the police interrogations, Dikshant was asked why he had not run away from Priya, as soon as he came to know about her real business venture. Dikshant was quoted as saying that he tried to leave but did not find the right opportunity.

Now this could be Dikshant cleaning his tracks and pretending to be a mere accomplice rather than the perpetrator in the hope that the press sympathizes with him and Priya takes the complete brunt of the punishment. Or he could be telling the truth. But it is a half-truth because the 'right' opportunity he refers to was never in contention.

It was his greed and hope that Priya would help erase his debt that made him stay on with her.

Honey trapping and blackmailing is one level of crime. Cold-blooded murder is the ultimate, heinous offence!

What began, as a honey trap ended up in murder. But who do you blame as being the mastermind?

Priya, who was already a criminal but was now being mentally pressurized to pull off this kidnapping? Never before in her modus operandi had she kidnapped anybody. She knew the sum required to erase Dikshant's debt was large and only a ransom paid in one shot would solve the problem or perhaps this time, Priya's greed had gotten the better of her.

Or, Dikshant the whiner? After all, he had kept nagging Priya about the debt that he had. He was the one who planted the motive. And Priya responded like a faithful lover, trying to solve the problem at hand. Because the intention and motive both play a very important role when it comes to judging a crime in the court of law.

- Rashmi Singh writes, 'Actus non facit reum nisi men sit rea' is a well-known principle of natural justice, which means that an act alone does not make a man guilty unless accompanied by a guilty intention. Therefore, the combination of an act and an intent (that is guilty) constitutes a crime. Merely an act cannot be considered a crime unless a particular guilty intent is associated and accompanied with it. Under the criminal law, the intention is seen as a deliberate cause and a willful effort to produce a particular consequence that is prohibited by law, whereas motive is the implicit cause that instigates a person to do any act or omit to do it.

While the intention is the objective behind a crime, the motive is the driving force that instigated or encouraged the accused to do it.

Intention helps determine whether the accused committed the act (of which he is accused) on purpose or by accident. Motive, on the other hand only answers the question that why the accused committed the crime.[65]

And in this case, both the intention and the motive nailed the three accused.

In July 2020, the Rajasthan High Court rejected the bail plea of Priya Seth. Priya and her lawyer had been attempting to paint a picture of innocence, where the duo claimed it wasn't Priya but her two friends who had committed the murder! Government lawyer Sher Singh Mahala, while opposing the bail, said that till March 2020, statements of 29 out of 41 witnesses had been taken. The flat where the murder took place was in the name of Priya Seth and it was she who had made the ransom call. Priya has a hand in befriending and calling the deceased. Pankaj Bhandari quashed the bail application.[66]

Deepika Narayan Bhardwaj took to Twitter (now X) and tweeted:

'Priya Seth denies killing her tinder date Dushyant Singh while seeking bail. Court rejects it. She had confessed to the killing in interview she gave me.'

Repost: #TheTinderMurder

The separate lawyers took turns in applying for bail. But the court was having none of it. On 19th February 2021, Jaipur High Court rejected the 3rd bail application of Dikshant Kamra. Pankaj Bhandari representing the Bench stated, 'Considering the contentions put forth by counsel for the State and counsel for the complainant, I am not inclined to entertain the third bail application.

In May 2022, Priya Seth applied for bail. Justice Pankaj Bhandari promptly rejected it.[67] By this time, she had already been in jail for four years while her trial continued. The court agreed that it is a serious case of murder, and therefore the accused cannot be given the benefit of bail. Secondly, forty-four of the forty-five witnesses, including testimonies from investigating officer Gur Bhoopendra Singh, were taken and cross-examined as well, and the court was nearing giving the verdict. And therefore, again, the accused could not be released on bail.

Days after the murder, when Dushyant's mother Vaijanti was interviewed, she was clearly in denial. The heart of the mother could not accept the truth about her son, and she said, 'My son was simple and straightforward. No mischief.'[68]

On Instagram @rockydikshant describes himself as 'Dikshaant Kamra (Rocky) might be a sinner and I might be a saint' on his profile.[69] On Facebook, for a long time, the last post was made on 28 April 2018, just four days before the kidnapping. The post was about 'Do you believe in long distance relationships?'[70]

The remnants of the Bollywood dream that Dikshant Kamra once pursued can still be seen on YouTube, where a casting director has uploaded one of his auditions. Ironically, in the clip he is playing the role of a rogue who with a smirk on his face directs his cronies, '*Zara thanedaar saab ko batayengay nahi hum hai kaun, aur karte kya hai?* (Won't you tell the police inspector who I am and what I do?) And he follows this with another dialogue warning the cop to stay away from his criminal business or else '*mujhe do minute nahi lagengay tumhari photo par phoolon ki maala chadhane me!*' (It will not take me two minutes to kill you and for your photo-frame to have a garland!)[71]

Did Dikshant know at this point in his life that he was not just giving an audition but also manifesting his own future?

On 18 October 2023, the district judge court in Jaipur announced that the final arguments between prosecution and defense had been completed and that the court was likely to give its verdict in the case on 26 October 2023.

A four-year-old exile and the end of an epic battle in which Ravana was defeated was followed by the homecoming of Lord Ram, his wife Sita and brother Lakshman to Ayodhya. And for centuries, this event from the Ramayana has been celebrated in the northern part of India as Diwali.

Meanwhile, in southern India, Diwali commemorates Lord Krishna's triumph over the demon Narakasura. In the western regions, the festival signifies the moment when Lord Vishnu, the Preserver in the Hindu trinity, dispatched the demon King Bali to govern the netherworld. The stories may be different, but the outcome is the same. Diwali marks the victory of good against evil.

In 2023, twelve days after Diwali was celebrated, the Jaipur Court was ready with its verdict. It was time once again for evil to be decimated by all that is good.

Sessions judge Ajit Kumar Hinger declared that the prosecution has presented adequate evidence to authenticate the facts pertaining to the case. The evidence presented by the prosecution proves that the accused have committed the crime.

Based on the evidence, the court convicted the three accused under sections 342 (wrongful confinement), 302 (murder), 201 (causing disappearance of evidence of offence) and 120-B (criminal conspiracy) of the Indian Penal Code and sentenced them to life imprisonment.

The ringleader, Priya Seth, and her paramour Dikshant Kamra were in judicial custody and therefore did not appear at court when the district judge convicted them. The third accused, Lakshya Walia, was present in court. He too was taken into judicial custody.[72]

Afterword

Cautionary Tales

Every day the clock resets. Every day is a new day. Every day we are a day older. Nothing remains constant. One would think that the modus operandi employed by Priya Seth, which became 'Breaking News' on television channels across India in 2018 would now be 'outed' and 'spotted' by alert social media users, and thereby, they will not fall into the same trap. WRONG!! The modus operandi keeps on evolving and our endorphin-craving selves keep making the same mistake again and again. We humans are supposedly the smartest species on the planet. I doubt it.

2018, Delhi: Imagine how surprised Hema (name changed) must have been when she saw her boyfriend's wedding photos on Facebook. She had met Hemant (name changed) on Facebook and they had fallen in love. The next logical decision was to move in together.

Unknown to Hema, when her boyfriend once travelled to his native village in Himachal Pradesh, it is not a routine 'Namaste, Mummy-Papa' visit. He had, in fact, gone to marry the girl his parents had chosen for him. Caught between his libido and honesty, he then decided to have the best of both worlds and continued being with both women: his wife and girlfriend. But 'shit always hits the fan' (old jungle saying). And it did when one of Hemant's enthu friends tagged him in a photo from his wedding on Facebook. Hema confronted Hemant, who ending up killing Hema. Hemant ran away only to be caught later.

2018, Haldwani: Neha Sen had always been a tomboy who loved the good life. And to have it, she was willing to do anything, including pretending to be a man. So she created a Facebook profile as Krishna Sen. Krishna started befriending women online and ended up marrying two of them. It is not just the women she managed to deceive but the entire town, where the people all believed in the well-crafted illusion! In 2014, Sen travelled to Haldwani's Kathgodam region to meet a woman she had befriended online, posing as the son of an Aligarh businessman. They married that year, but Sen allegedly subjected Kamini, holding two master's degrees, to physical abuse for dowry and extracted Rs 8.5 lakh from her family. Kamini revealed to news agency ANI that after their marriage, Sen behaved aggressively, engaging in drinking, smoking and verbal abuse, even threatening harm after marrying another woman.

Two years later, Sen enticed another woman from Uttarakhand's Kaladhungi town and entered into matrimony with her in April 2016. The 'second wife,' identified as Nisha, had attended Sen's first wedding as a guest. Sen rented a room in the Tikoniya area of Haldwani and accommodated both 'wives' there, according to the police.

Post the 'marriages,' Sen reportedly prohibited the women from seeing her bare body or having physical contact, relying on sex toys to consummate the relationships, as per police statements. A subsequent medical examination affirmed Sen's biological status as a woman, as stated by Khanduri.

'The girl from Kaladhungi eventually discovered that Krishna was not a man, but Sen convinced her to remain silent by promising financial incentives. The girl from Kathgodam lodged a report with the Haldwani Police, alleging dowry demands and threats, leading to Sen's arrest,' Khanduri explained.[73]

2018, Chittorgarh/Lucknow: In Lucknow, a woman connected with another woman from Chittorgarh, and as they engaged in conversation, they discovered striking similarities—they were both in their mid-twenties, held government jobs (one as a clerk and the other as a nurse) and had recently married businessmen. As they shared photos of their husbands on WhatsApp, the shocking revelation unfolded—they were both married to the same man! This man, it turned out, preyed on women in government service, capitalizing on their stable incomes. The discovery marked the intersection of their lives in an unexpected and unsettling manner. And this led to the opening of not a 'cat with nine lives', but 'a man with nine wives'.

Sameer Khan had a knack for collecting wedding vows like some people collect paintings or Pokémon cards!

The drama unfolded when the alleged ninth wife, who met Khan on an online matrimonial site, discovered she was just one entry in Khan's bridal sweepstakes.

According to the woman's complaint to the police, she encountered Khan, a resident of Chittorgarh district in Rajasthan, on an online matrimonial site. After their marriage in 2016, Khan relocated to Lucknow, where the couple began residing in a rented apartment.

The woman's decision to involve the police stemmed from her discovery of Khan's two additional marriages. Expressing her suspicion of his involvement in extramarital affairs, she highlighted his frequent and lengthy conversations with unknown women over the phone.

Over time, her suspicions deepened, prompting her to take matters further and initiate a more in-depth inquiry. The police investigation revealed that Sameer, the accused, had previously been married to a woman named Neha, with whom he had three children. To add another layer to the complexity, Khan went on to marry another woman called Yasmeen in February of 2018. The twist in the tale was when Yasmeen reached out to the Lucknow woman on Facebook, disclosing her own marital connection with Khan, as disclosed by Dubey.[74]

Bengaluru, February 2023: And this is one of the latest modus operandi. A girl calls you on a WhatsApp video call. As you speak, she suddenly strips naked and screenshots you or video records the screen. This makes you look like a willing participant to this 'sex act.' Next, you start getting calls and messages threatening to make the video public. In February 2023, a UK-based software engineer found himself ensnared in a web of deceit spun by a woman he encountered on a matrimonial site. Then during a video call, she stripped while recording the interaction. This was followed by blackmail and threats.

Faced with impending public humiliation, the man transferred a staggering sum of Rs 1.14 crore to her! When the woman insisted on more money, the techie reported to the police and managed to recover Rs 80 lakh. But the woman remained at large.[75]

New Delhi, March 2023: The Noida Police apprehended six foreign nationals who exploited dating apps such as Bumble, Tinder, Hinge and OkCupid to deceive unsuspecting women. Originating from Delta State in Nigeria, the five men came to India in 2021 with educational and medical visas. A surprising twist unfolded as a Bhutanese woman from Trongsa married one of the accused and became an unexpected member, revealing a complex web of international relationships.

The group, posing as doctors from countries such as the Netherlands and the US, would chat with women on these dating sites and make them believe they were truly interested in them. They would later concoct a story of being detained by Indian customs officials upon arrival with a significant sum in foreign currency. The gang members would then ask the women for help and convince them to forward some money with promises of repayment. Unfortunately, the assurances were a facade, leaving defrauded women to grapple with the realization of falling victim to a well-orchestrated scam.[76]

According to an *India Today* article published on 14 November 2023, there has been an increase of scams on dating sites like Bumble and Tinder.[77]

This evolving landscape of cybercrime emphasizes the scary intersection of technology and deception. As the number of dating sites increase every day, more and more people register with them, increasing the number of fraudsters waiting to exploit this basic human need for love and connections.

According to author Shreya Gupta in her article 'Modern Love: India's Dating Industry' for website smallcase.com reveals these staggering figures and statistics:[78]

India is the fifth fastest-growing dating app market in the world as users spend millions every year.

Indian consumers spent $9.9 million up to December 2022 on dating and friendship apps up from $4.5 million compared to the same period last year.

Currently, dating apps reach 2.2 per cent of India's total population, with projections of 3.6 per cent by 2024, according to industry surveys.

According to Statista.com, the online dating segment's turnover in India is expected to reach $783 million by 2024 from $454 million in 2021.[79]

We can say roughly 20 million Indians used dating apps just six years ago. This figure surged by a massive 293 per cent since then and hit 82.4 million in 2023. The surge in usage is especially strong outside metro cities, which now account for 70 per cent of users of the dating apps such as Tinder, Bumble and TrulyMadly.[70]

Indians prefer Chamet, followed by Bumble, and then Tinder.

Revenue in the dating services market is projected to reach $402.10 million in 2024.[80] India will become the world's second-largest dating services market by 2027, with roughly 35 million more users than the US.

In the online dating market, the number of users is expected to amount to 29.2 million by 2029.[81]

And these are amazing numbers for the corporations that own the apps. With the almost impossible task of weeding out fake profiles before damage is done, and policing every account, it is the user who needs to be super-cautious.

Online Dating: Steps and Measures to Protect Yourself

You should hopefully be safe from scams and fraudsters on dating sites if you take a few precautionary steps and measures that I have collated from various sites.

I have shared tips like these across various episodes of *Savdhaan India*, addressing cybercrime and dating app scams. This television show, which I conceived in 2012 and then produced for the next seven years, has garnered positive feedback from viewers, who found these insights valuable.

1. Exercise caution in sharing personal information. Refrain from disclosing your home address or phone number to individuals you have recently connected with on dating apps, as this information could potentially be misused.
2. Avoid sending money to online acquaintances. Regardless of how compelling their narrative may be, resist the urge to send money to someone you have never met face to face.
3. Be wary of financial requests. If someone solicits money from you, treat it as a significant warning sign of potential scamming activity.
4. Conduct a reverse image search on profile pictures. Utilize this tool to verify if the images are being used elsewhere on the internet, helping you assess the authenticity of the profile.
5. Perform a Google search on the person's name. This search may reveal any concerning information or red flags associated with the individual in question.[82]

RAINN (Rape, Abuse and Incest National Network), which is USA's largest anti-sexual violence organization, advises that when we meet someone new, whether online or offline, it's wise to keep a few safety precautions in mind. Dating apps don't conduct criminal background checks on users, so it's up to each user to determine if they are comfortable meeting up with someone.

6. Use different photos for your dating profile so that when the attackers do a reverse Google image search, it does not compromise your personal details or ancillary information. Do not connect your social media accounts to your dating account. Also put different photographs on each or else it will be easier for someone to find you on social media.

7. Avoid connecting with suspicious profiles. If the person you matched with has no bio or linked social media accounts, and has only posted one picture, it may be a fake account. It is a red flag!

8. Do a search on your potential date across social media sites. If you know your match's name or handles on social media—or better yet if you have mutual friends online—look them up and make sure they aren't 'catfishing' you by using a fake social media account to create their dating profile. Also swipe only verified profiles.

9. Block and report suspicious users. You can block and report another user if you feel their profile is suspicious or if they have acted inappropriately towards you.

10. When on Instagram, click on the account and go to 'About this account'. Here, you will find the date when the person joined Instagram—a recent date is a red flag. If they message you, go to 'About this account' and see where the account is based in, and also former usernames. You will see how many times the account has changed their usernames. If they have done it multiple times over a short period of time, it is a red flag.

11. Scammers usually will lean on a sob story to win your trust and sympathy, only to manipulate your emotions and get you to do things. Beware of these award-winning notorious stories:
    - Asks for money due to a personal crisis: customs, money stolen, parents are ill, credit card not working or lost or stolen—you get the drift!
    - Claims to be from your country but is currently living, working or travelling abroad and is in a personal crisis.
    - Claims to be recently widowed with children.
    - Disappears suddenly from the site and then reappears under a different name.
    - Gives vague answers to specific questions.
    - Overly complimentary and romantic too early in your communication.
    - Pressurizes you to provide your phone number or talk outside the dating app or site.
    - Requests your home or work address under the guise of sending flowers or gifts.
    - Tells inconsistent or grandiose stories.

- Uses disjointed language, bad grammar and spelling mistakes and yet the profile bio mentions a high level of education.

According to Mashable India:[83]

12. Do not sign up with a dating app using a social media account like Facebook or Instagram. You can sign up for Bumble with your phone number, while for apps like Tinder, Hinge and OkCupid, you can sign up with a phone number or email.

13. Mashable India echoes RAINN's advice, cautioning against signing up with social media due to the potential exchange of data between platforms. For example, if you register using your Instagram account, your matches may appear as suggested people to follow. Although it might be enticing to streamline your profile setup through a social platform, this convenience facilitates the sharing of data.

Tim Maliyil, founder of encryption and mobile security service AlertBoot, emphasizes that connecting Instagram to your profile provides Meta with all the necessary data points to link these individuals together on Instagram.

The next step is even more dangerous, and one has to be extra cautious. This is when you take the date from the virtual space to the real world; when you decide to meet in person. If you are scared, that's good; it means that you will take safety precautions and not take things for granted. Remember, you have a family that loves you and would not want any kind of harm to happen to you.

Here are some recommendations from RAINN.[84]

1. **Video chat before meeting someone in person**
   - Schedule a video chat before the in-person meeting to verify the match's identity.
   - Resistance to a video call should raise suspicions.
2. **Inform a friend**
   - Share your date's profile screenshot with a friend.
   - Notify a friend of your date's location and any changes during the date.
   - Arrange to check in partway through the date or upon returning home.
3. **Choose public venues**
   - Opt for public places such as cafes, restaurants or bars for the initial meetings.
   - Avoid isolated locations or private settings, prioritizing safety for both parties.
4. **Independent transportation**
   - Arrange your own transportation to and from the date.
   - Avoid getting into a vehicle with someone unfamiliar, even if offered.
   - Keep ride-share apps, a charged phone and a back-up charger handy.
5. **Alcohol and drugs**
   - Be mindful of alcohol consumption and set personal limits.
   - Refrain from using drugs, as they may alter perceptions or interact unexpectedly with the alcohol.

6. **Seek assistance if uncomfortable**
   - Enlist the help of bartenders or staff at the restaurant if you are feeling uncomfortable.
   - They can create a distraction, call for help or arrange a safe ride home.
7. **Trust your instincts**
   - Trust your instincts. If you feel uneasy, feel free to leave the date or cut off communication.
   - Prioritize personal safety over politeness.
8. **Post-date actions**
   - Unmatch, block or report if uncomfortable or unsafe during the date.
   - Restrict access to your profile for added security in the future.

When you are a victim, this is what you can do:

Reporting Cyber Crime in India

National Contact Helpline 1930

Dial 1930 for the national cybercrime helpline. If you become a victim of financial fraud, provide essential details, including your name, contact information, account number, and specifics of the recipient account.

Online Complaint Filing:
Report cybercrimes against women and children or any cybercrime at https://cybercrime.gov.in/ File a report anonymously if needed.

Ensure you have necessary documents, such as your bank account number, recipient account details, and the linked contact number. Track your complaint status post-filing.

For anonymous complaints, omit personal details but provide comprehensive incident/complaint information for police action. Register using your mobile number, receive a One Time Password (OTP), and report the complaint.

The National Cyber Crime Reporting Portal has a page that helpfully provides the contact details of the State/UT Nodal Officer and Grievance Officer. You can visit it here: https://cybercrime.gov.in/Webform/Crime_NodalGrivanceList.aspx

Complaint Handling

Complaints on the portal are managed by State/UT police authorities. Upon submission, receive a confirmation message in the portal. For 'Report and Track' or 'Report Other Cybercrime' submissions, get an SMS and email with a complaint reference number.

Contact Local Police Station

If online or helpline reporting is challenging, visit the nearest police station to file a complaint. Police officials will handle the case and transfer it to the cyber cell.

Additional Helpline Numbers

National police helpline number: 112
National women helpline number: 181
Toll-free police control room number: 100

If you have enjoyed reading the book, I humbly request you to please visit the Amazon and the Goodreads page for the book and leave your rating and review. Readers' feedback and appreciation always encourages authors to go on. Thanks.

Acknowledgements

First, and most importantly, I would like to thank the Rajasthan Police and Station House Officer (SHO) Gur Bhoopendra Singh and his team for allowing me to tell this story. Without their generous participation and insights, this book would not have been possible.

I want to thank Gurveen Chadha at Penguin Random House India (PRHI). This marks our third true-crime collaboration! I also want to thank Anushree Kaushal and Manali Das from PRHI for seeing this book through.

I want to thank my legal friends who helped me with translations of the legal documents: Siddharth S. Upadhyay, Advocate K. Swati, Naman D. Bajhal and Advocate Shyam R. Jaiswal.

Thank you to my friend Dr Siddharth Nirwan and his wife Mahima Panwar, who made my trips to Jaipur feel like I was going back home. Thank you for the fun, food and long drives! And, most importantly, helping me get in touch with Gur Bhoopendra Singh.

Thank you to journalist Deepika Narayan Bhardwaj, who gave the world the first glimpse of Priya Seth, Dikshant Kamra and Lakshya Walia.

Thank you to my literary agent, Suhail Mathur of The Book Bakers. It was providence that we met out of the blue and you helped me begin my literary journey. Your input and guidance are always appreciated. May the force be with you, always!

I remember reading about the case when it happened, and later, being completely stunned as I watched the video shot by journalist Deepika Narayan Bhardwaj. There was something about the case that fascinated me. It was not the crime but the people behind it that got me interested. Having studied serial killers closely for my first book, *The Deadly Dozen*, where I went into their heads to decipher their thought process, I wanted to find out what was inside the heads of the trio who committed this crime. And so here we are . . .

I hope you have enjoyed this journey into the minds of the Jaipur Tinder Killers.

Anirban Bhattacharyya	**Gur Bhoopendra Singh** 2018: SHO, Jhotwara, Jaipur 2024: SHO, Manak Chowk, Jaipur (North)
Rajasthan Police	**Priya Seth**
Rajasthan Police	**Dikshant Kamra**
Rajasthan Police	**Lakshya Walia**

Notes

1 'Check out the Indian names that get the most right swipes', GQ, 20 December 2016, https://www.gqindia.com/content/check-indian-names-get-right-swipes (accessed 25 June 2024).

2 Have changed her name to Neha, as that is the alias mentioned in the charge sheet. Neha was an imagined name. Also, in this article, it clearly says she used fake names on tinder: 'Priya scanned dating sites to blackmail wealthy men', 6 May 2018, *Times of India*, https://timesofindia.indiatimes.com/city/jaipur/priya-scanned-dating-sites-to-blackmail-wealthy-men/articleshow/64046550.cms (accessed 25 June 2024).

3 Neha Seth was a pseudonym that Priya used to create a fake profile on Tinder.

4 This article clearly mentions the hotel near Jawahar Circle as one of her chosen places. Santosh Trivedi, 'वेश्यावृत्ति से जुड़ी साइट्स पर अपना मोबाइल नम्बर छोड़ देती थी प्रिया सेठ, रकम लेती और भाग जाती' (Priya Seth used to leave her mobile number on prostitution related sites, take the money and run away), Patrika, 5 May 2018, https://www.patrika.com/jaipur-news/dushyantsharma-

murder-know-all-about-priya-seth-2754865
(accessed 20 June 2024).

5 The amount is mentioned in these articles:
Santosh Trivedi, 'वेश्यावृत्ति से जुड़ी साइट्स पर अपना
मोबाइल नम्बर छोड़ देती थी प्रिया सेठ, रकम लेती और भाग जाती'
(Priya Seth used to leave her mobile number on
prostitution related sites, take the money and run away),
Patrika, 5 May 2018, https://www.patrika.com/
jaipur-news/dushyantsharma-murder-know-all-
about-priya-seth-2754865 (accessed 20 June 2024)
and Snigdha Poonam, 'Greed, deceit and lies: How a
Tinder date ended in murder', *Hindustan Times*, 25
September 2018, https://www.hindustantimes.com/
india-news/a-true-account-of-a-tinder-murder/
story-NA4xQ19l42XNwjVb3BpZzK.html (accessed
25 February 2024).

6 Snigdha Poonam, 'Greed, deceit and lies: How
a Tinder date ended in murder', *Hindustan Times*,
25 September 2018, https://www.hindustantimes.
com/india-news/a-true-account-of-a-tinder-murder/
story-NA4xQ19l42XNwjVb3BpZzK.html (accessed
25 February 2024).

7 Snigdha Poonam, 'Greed, deceit and lies: How
a Tinder date ended in murder', *Hindustan Times*,
25 September 2018, https://www.hindustantimes.
com/india-news/a-true-account-of-a-tinder-
murder/story-NA4xQ19l42XNwjVb3BpZzK.html
(accessed 25 February 2024).

8 Snigdha Poonam, 'Greed, deceit and lies: How
a Tinder date ended in murder', *Hindustan Times*,
25 September 2018, https://www.hindustantimes.

com/india-news/a-true-account-of-a-tinder-murder/story-NA4xQ19l42XNwjVb3BpZzK.html (accessed 25 February 2024).

9   'Tinder date killing: Police probing if Priya Seth's boyfriend has criminal history', *Hindustan Times*, 8 May 2018, https://www.hindustantimes.com/jaipur/tinder-date-killing-police-probing-if-priya-seth-s-boyfriend-has-criminal-history/story-2jzHfxqmiwgGO5seY9rKcO.html (accessed 28 February 2024).

10 Snigdha Poonam, 'Greed, deceit and lies: How a Tinder date ended in murder', *Hindustan Times*, 25 September 2018, https://www.hindustantimes.com/india-news/a-true-account-of-a-tinder-murder/story-NA4xQ19l42XNwjVb3BpZzK.html (accessed 29 February 2024).

11 Snigdha Poonam, 'Greed, deceit and lies: How a Tinder date ended in murder', *Hindustan Times*, 25 September 2018, https://www.hindustantimes.com/india-news/a-true-account-of-a-tinder-murder/story-NA4xQ19l42XNwjVb3BpZzK.html (accessed 29 February 2024).

12 Snigdha Poonam, 'Greed, deceit and lies: How a Tinder date ended in murder', *Hindustan Times*, 25 September 2018, https://www.hindustantimes.com/india-news/a-true-account-of-a-tinder-murder/story-NA4xQ19l42XNwjVb3BpZzK.html (accessed 29 February 2024).

13 Snigdha Poonam, 'Greed, deceit and lies: How a Tinder date ended in murder', *Hindustan Times*, 25 September 2018, https://www.hindustantimes.com/india-news/a-true-account-of-a-tinder-murder/

story-NA4xQ19l42XNwjVb3BpZzK.html   (accessed 29 February 2024).

14   Snigdha Poonam, 'Greed, deceit and lies: How a Tinder date ended in murder', *Hindustan Times*, 25 September 2018, https://www.hindustantimes. com/india-news/a-true-account-of-a-tinder-murder/ story-NA4xQ19l42XNwjVb3BpZzK.html   (accessed 24 March 2024).

15   Nitika Kakkar, Murder, 'ATM loot, extortion: 27-year-old Jaipur woman accused of killing man she lured on Tinder', *Hindustan Times*, 7 March 2018, https:// www.hindustantimes.com/india-news/murder-atm-loot-extortion-the-life-of-a-27-year-old-jaipur-woman-accused-of-killing-man-she-lured-on-tinder/ story-LtIw9lf2dl7wjVC3Num8mO.html (accessed 29 February 2024).

16   'Woman threatens to frame man in fake rape case, held', *Times of India*, 9 March 2018, https://timesofindia. indiatimes.com/city/jaipur/woman-threatens-to-frame-man-in-fake-rape-case-held/articleshow/ 63224312.cms (accessed 29 February 2024).

17   Singdha Poonam, 'Greed, deceit and lies: How a Tinder date ended in murder', *Hindustan Times*, 25 September 2018, https://www.hindustantimes.com/ india-news/a-true-account-of-a-tinder-murder/story-NA4xQ19l42XNwjVb3BpZzK.html   (accessed 29 February 2024).

18   'Woman, boyfriend held for trying to loot ATM in Jaipur', *Times of India*, 1 December 2014.

19   'Woman, boyfriend held for trying to loot ATM in Jaipur', *Times of India*, 1 December 2014.

20   'Woman, boyfriend held for trying to loot ATM in
      Jaipur', *Times of India*, 1 December 2014.

21   'Police arrest two for attempting to break open ATM
      in Jaipur', Zee News, 30 November 2014, https://
      zeenews.india.com/news/rajasthan/police-arrest-two-
      for-attempting-to-break-open-atm-in-jaipur_1507104.
      html (accessed 1 March 2024).

22   Snigdha Poonam, 'Greed, deceit and lies: How a
      Tinder date ended in murder', *Hindustan Times*, 25
      September 2018, https://www.hindustantimes.com/
      india-news/a-true-account-of-a-tinder-murder/story-
      NA4xQ19l42XNwjVb3BpZzK.html   (accessed   20
      June 2024).

23   This article mentions the case as well as the only article that
      reveals the name of the ex-boyfriend as Gurujar Singh:
      Pranav Kumar, 'Priya Seth: Meet The Lady Who Killed
      Her Tinder Date and Cheated Thousands', VoxSpace, 7
      July 2018, https://www.voxspace.in/2018/07/07/priya-
      seth/ (accessed 25 June 2024).

24   'Woman threatens to frame man in fake rape case, held',
      Times of India, 9 March 2018, https://timesofindia.
      indiatimes.com/city/jaipur/woman-threatens-to-frame-
      man-in-fake-rape-case-held/articleshow/63224312.cms
      (accessed 20 June 2024).

25   Vikram and Betaal is derived from *Betaal Pachisi*, an
      enchanting collection penned by the eleventh-century
      Kashmiri poet Somdev Bhatt.

26   'Woman threatens to frame man in fake rape
      case, held', *Times of India*, 9 March 2018, https://
      timesofindia.indiatimes.com/city/jaipur/woman-

threatens-to-frame-man-in-fake-rape-case-held/
articleshow/63224312.cms.

27   'Jaipur gang which extorted around Rs 15 crore
     from fake rape cases busted', *Hindustan Times*,
     25 December 2016, https://www.hindustantimes.com/
     india-news/jaipur-gang-which-extorted-around-rs-15-
     crore-from-fake-rape-cases-busted/story-vyQtaSJhmIc
     Wsz2rF4DnJI.html (accessed 24 March 2024).

28   'Jaipur gang which extorted around Rs 15 crore from fake
     rape cases busted', *Hindustan Times*, 25 December 2016,
     https://www.hindustantimes.com/india-news/jaipur-
     gang-which-extorted-around-rs-15-crore-from-fake-rape-
     cases-busted/story-vyQtaSJhmIcWsz2rF4DnJI.html
     (accessed 2 March 2024).

29   '21-year-old DJ runs away with Rs 1 crore, caught after
     going live on Facebook', *India Today*, 18 March 2017,
     https://www.indiatoday.in/fyi/story/dj-adaa-shikha-
     tiwari-lucknow-honey-trapping-doctor-crore-977514-
     2017-05-17 (accessed 2 March 2024).

30   'Honeytrap case: Accused aspired to become TV anchor',
     Times of India, 18 May 2017, https://timesofindia.
     indiatimes.com/city/jaipur/girl-aspired-to-become-
     television-anchor-urge-for-easy-money-made-her-to-
     be-part-of-extortion-gang/articleshow/58722296.cms
     (accessed 2 March 2024).

31   'Hong Kong-born NRI arrested for alleged involvement
     in sex racket', *Times of India*, 7 January 2017, https://
     timesofindia.indiatimes.com/india/hong-kong-born-
     nri-arrested-for-alleged-involvement-in-sex-racket/
     articleshow/56384932.cms (accessed 2 March 2024).

32   'Woman threatens to frame man in fake rape
     case, held', *Times of India*, 9 March 2018, https://

timesofindia.indiatimes.com/city/jaipur/woman-threatens-to-frame-man-in-fake-rape-case-held/articleshow/63224312.cms (accessed 2 March 2024).

33   Deepika Narayan Bhardwaj, 'The Tinder Murder: How Priya Seth murdered her Tinder Date and cheated thousands of Men', YouTube, https://www.youtube.com/watch?v=ICYE358tA9Y (accessed 25 June 2024).

34   Deepika Narayan Bhardwaj, 'The Tinder Murder: How Priya Seth murdered her Tinder Date and cheated thousands of Men', YouTube, https://www.youtube.com/watch?v=ICYE358tA9Y (accessed 25 June 2024).

35   Nitika Kakkar, 'Murder, ATM loot, extortion: 27-year-old Jaipur woman accused of killing man she lured on Tinder', *Hindustan Times*, 7 March 2018, https://www.hindustantimes.com/india-news/murder-atm-loot-extortion-the-life-of-a-27-year-old-jaipur-woman-accused-of-killing-man-she-lured-on-tinder/story-LtIw 9lf2dl7wjVC3Num8mO.html (accessed 2 March 2024).

36   Deepika Narayan Bhardwaj, 'The Tinder Murder: How Priya Seth murdered her Tinder Date and cheated thousands of Men', YouTube, https://www.youtube.com/watch?v=ICYE358tA9Y (accessed 25 June 2024).

37   'Priya and Kamra wanted to marry each other: Rajasthan police', *Hindustan Times*, 16 May 2018, https://www.hindustantimes.com/jaipur/priya-and-kamra-wanted-to-marry-each-other-rajasthan-police/story-mDq8ZD8GyxYtR1xUzhFOSO.html (accessed 2 March 2024).

38   Deepika Narayan Bhardwaj, 'The Tinder Murder: How Priya Seth murdered her Tinder Date and cheated thousands of Men', YouTube, https://www.youtube.com/watch?v=ICYE358tA9Y (accessed 25 June 2024).

39   Santosh Trivedi, 'वेश्यावृत्ति से जुड़ी साइट्स पर अपना मोबाइल
     नम्बर छोड़ देती थी प्रिया सेठ, रकम लेती और भाग जाती' (Priya Seth
     used to leave her mobile number on prostitution related
     sites, take the money and run away), Patrika, 5 May
     2018, https://www.patrika.com/jaipur-news/dushyant-
     sharma-murder-know-all-about-priya-seth-2754865
     (accessed 20 June 2024).

40   'Tinder date killing: Police probing if Priya Seth's boyfriend
     has criminal history', *Hindustan Times*, 8 May 2018,
     https://www.hindustantimes.com/jaipur/tinder-date-
     killing-police-probing-if-priya-seth-s-boyfriend-has-
     criminal-history/story-2jzHfxqmiwgGO5seY9rKcO.
     html (accessed 20 June 2024).

41   Aravind Balakrishnan, 'Tinder Date Gone Wrong:
     A Shocking Story of How a Woman Murdered Her
     Date', *Medium*, 1 January 2022, https://medium.com/
     illumination/tinder-date-gone-wrong-a-shocking-story-
     of-how-a-woman-murdered-her-date-ba3d7fe9584e
     (accessed 20 June 2024).

42   'Life sentence for 2 accused in Meenakshi Thapa
     murder case', *Asian Age*, 12 May 2018, https://www.
     asianage.com/metros/mumbai/120518/life-sentence-
     for-2-accused-in-meenakshi-thapa-murder-case.html
     (accessed 24 March 2024).

43   Snigdha Poonam, 'How a Tinder date in Jaipur ended
     in heartbreak and murder', Print, 23 Septmeber 2023,
     https://theprint.in/india/governance/how-a-tinder-
     date-in-jaipur-ended-in-heartbreak-and-murder/123087/
     (accessed 20 June 2024).

44   Deepika Narayan Bhardwaj, 'The Tinder Murder:
     How Priya Seth murdered her Tinder Date and
     cheated thousands of Men', YouTube, https://

www.youtube.com/watch?v=ICYE358tA9Y&t=19s (accessed 20 June 2024).

45 Aravind Balakrishnan, 'Tinder Date Gone Wrong: A Shocking Story of How a Woman Murdered Her Date', Medium.com, 1 January 2022, https://medium.com/illumination/tinder-date-gone-wrong-a-shocking-story-of-how-a-woman-murdered-her-date-ba3d7fe9584e (accessed 3 March 2024).

46 'Kidnapping case solved, four arrested', *Times of India*, 24 December 2002, https://timesofindia.indiatimes.com/city/delhi/kidnapping-case-solved-four-arrested/articleshow/32296084.cms (accessed 24 March 2024).

47 A translation of the original found in Aphorism #183 toward the end of Chapter IV in 'Beyond Good and Evil' In the original, it is 'Nicht daß du mich belogst, sondern daß ich dir nicht mehr glaube, hat mich erschüttert.'

48 A dicky is a colloquial term for the trunk or boot of a car, which is the covered space at the back of the vehicle where you can store luggage. The term is used in some regions, particularly in South Asia. In Indian English, the dicky is also known as the boot. The word 'dickey' comes from the British word for the American rumble seat that folded into the back of a pre-World War two-seater car.

49 Bharat Yadav and Manju Yadav, 'Domestic and Foreign Tourists Trends in Rajasthan 2010–19: A Survey', *International Journal of Research in Engineering, IT and Social Sciences*, Vol. 11, No. 7, July 2021, pp. 1–7. https://www.indusedu.org/pdfs/IJREISS/IJREISS_3794_75145.pdf (accessed 20 June 2024).

50 According to Section 302 of the Indian Penal Code, whoever kills any person, shall be punished with death

or imprisonment for life, as well as with fine. It is a non-bailable and cognizable offense.

51   You can read the story in *The Deadly Dozen: India's Most Notorious Serial Killers* (Gurugram: Penguin Random House India, 2019).

52   'Mumbai: How Alex Fialho nabbed dreaded serial killer Raman Raghav', *Mid-Day*, 16 November 2020, https://www.mid-day.com/mumbai/mumbai-news/article/mumbai-how-alex-fialho-nabbed-dreaded-serial-killer-raman-raghav-23092240 (accessed 24 March 2024).

53   Snigdha Poonam, 'Greed, deceit and lies: How a Tinder date ended in murder', *Hindustan Times*, 25 September 2018, https://www.hindustantimes.com/india-news/a-true-account-of-a-tinder-murder/story-NA4xQ19l42XNwjVb3BpZzK.html (accessed 24 March 2024).

54   Bharat Vasani and Varun Kannan, 'Supreme Court on the admissibility of electronic evidence under Section 65B of the Evidence Act', Cyril Amarchand Mangaldas, 27 January 2021, https://corporate.cyrilamarchandblogs.com/2021/01/supreme-court-on-the-admissibility-of-electronic-evidence-under-section-65b-of-the-evidence-act/ (accessed 24 March 2024).

55   Snigdha Poonam, 'Greed, deceit and lies: How a Tinder date ended in murder', *Hindustan Times*, 25 September 2018, https://www.hindustantimes.com/india-news/a-true-account-of-a-tinder-murder/story-NA4xQ19l42XNwjVb3BpZzK.html (accessed 6 March 2024).

56   Hematoma, pooling of blood in tissues or spaces outside the blood vessels that results when a vessel is cut or torn, such as through injury or other forms of

trauma. Blood and other fluids leak from the damaged vessel and collect in a mass.

57 Asphyxia is a condition where the body has too little oxygen and too much carbon dioxide. It's usually caused by an interruption in breathing or an insufficient oxygen supply. Asphyxia can lead to unconsciousness and sometimes death.

58 Deepika Narayan Bhardwaj, 'The Tinder Murder: How Priya Seth murdered her Tinder Date and cheated thousands of Men', https://www.youtube.com/watch?v=ICYE358tA9Y (accessed 20 June 2024).

59 'How Important Is Motive, Preparation And Previous Or Subsequent Conduct Under Section 8 Of The Evidence Act?' https://www.legalservicesindia.com/law/article/1956/5/How-Important-Is-Motive-Preparation-And-Previous-Or-Subsequent-Conduct-Under-Section-8-Of-The-Evidence-Act- (accessed 20 June 2024).

60 Snigdha Poonam, 'Greed, deceit and lies: How a Tinder date ended in murder', *Hindustan Times*, 25 September 2018, https://www.hindustantimes.com/india-news/a-true-account-of-a-tinder-murder/story-NA4xQ19l42XNwjVb3BpZzK.html (accessed 6 March 2024).

61 Snigdha Poonam, 'Greed, deceit and lies: How a Tinder date ended in murder', *Hindustan Times*, 25 September 2018, https://www.hindustantimes.com/india-news/a-true-account-of-a-tinder-murder/story-NA4xQ19l42XNwjVb3BpZzK.html (accessed 6 March 2024).

62 Snigdha Poonam, 'Lady Killers', *Hindustan Times*, 24 December 2021, https://openthemagazine.com/cover-stories/lady-killers/ (accessed 6 March 2024).

63   Snigdha Poonam, 'Greed, deceit and lies: How a Tinder date ended in murder', *Hindustan Times*, 25 September 2018, https://www.hindustantimes. com/india-news/a-true-account-of-a-tinder-murder/ story-NA4xQ19l42XNwjVb3BpZzK.html (accessed 6 March 2024).

64   Snigdha Poonam, 'Greed, deceit and lies: How a Tinder date ended in murder', *Hindustan Times*, 25 September 2018, https://www.hindustantimes.com/ india-news/a-true-account-of-a-tinder-murder/ story-NA4xQ19l42XNwjVb3BpZzK.html (accessed 6 March 2024).

65   https://portal.theedulaw.com/SingleNotes?title= difference-between-intention-and-motive-importance- of-motive-in-law-of-crime

66   Pushpendra Shekhawat, 'शातिर हसीना ने कोर्ट में खेला बड़ा दांव, कहा: मैंने नहीं साथियों ने मारा, खुद को बताया बेकसूर' (The cunning beauty played a big trick in the court, said: I did not kill him but my friends did, she declared herself innocent), Patrika, 6 July 2020, https://www.patrika.com/jaipur-news/ dushyant-murder-mystery-accused-priya-seth-in-court- jaipur-6249008/ (accessed 24 March 2024).

67   'जयपुरः हनीट्रैप में फंसाकर मर्डर की आरोपी प्रिया सेठ की जमानत अर्जी खारिज', ZeeNews, 17 May 2022, https://zeenews. india.com/hindi/india/rajasthan/jaipur/jaipur-bail- application-of-priya-seth-accused-of-murder-by-being- implicated-in-honeytrap-rejected/1187920 (accessed 24 March 2024).

68   Snigdha Poonam, 'Greed, deceit and lies: How a Tinder date ended in murder', *Hindustan Times*, 25 September 2018, https://www.hindustantimes.com/ india-news/a-true-account-of-a-tinder-murder/

story-NA4xQ19l42XNwjVb3BpZzK.html (accessed 6 March 2024).

69   https://www.instagram.com/rockydikshant/

70   https://www.facebook.com/dikshant.kaamra

71   https://www.youtube.com/watch?v=08bwhiPFADA

72   'Honeytrap murder: Woman, two accomplices convicted', *Times of India*, 24 November 2023, https://timesofindia. indiatimes.com/city/jaipur/honeytrap-murder-woman-two-accomplices-convicted/articleshow/105459931.cms (accessed 24 March 2024).

73   Abhinav Madhwal, 'Woman poses as man, marries two women for dowry in Nainital', *Hindustan Times*, 16 February 2018, https://www.hindustantimes.com/ dehradun/woman-poses-as-man-marries-two-women-for-dowry-in-nainital/story-FrrrJgVCswyQvFRPDu TVdM.html (accessed 6 March 2024).

74   'Rajasthan man held for "fraudulently marrying" several women', *Hindustan Times*, 2 May 2018, https://www. hindustantimes.com/lucknow/lucknow-man-held-for-fraudulently-marrying-nine-women/story-O4Pqht4y 4olc8uWXqZXO2O.html (accessed 6 March 2024).

75   Divyanshi Verma, 'Techie gets blackmailed by woman he met on matrimonial site, loses Rs 1.1 crore after a video call', *India Today*, 1 August 2023, https://www. indiatoday.in/technology/news/story/techie-gets-blackmailed-by-woman-he-met-on-matrimonial-site-loses-rs-11-crore-after-a-video-call-2414743-2023-08-01 (accessed 6 March 2024).

76   Shobhit Gupta, 'Noida: 6 foreigners held for duping "hundreds" of women through dating apps', *Hindustan Times*, 5 March 2023, https://www.hindustantimes. com/cities/noida-news/noida-6-foreigners-held-

for-duping-hundreds-of-women-through-dating-apps-101678030238771.html (accessed 6 March 2024).

77 Divyanshi Sharma, 'Bumble and Tinder scam on rise: Here is how you can keep yourself safe on these dating apps', *India Today*, 14 November 2023, https://www.indiatoday.in/technology/news/story/bumble-and-tinder-scam-on-rise-here-is-how-you-can-keep-yourself-safe-on-these-dating-apps-2462741-2023-11-14 (accessed 6 March 2024).

78 Shreya Gupta, 'Modern Love: India's Dating Industry', small case, 4 August 2023, https://www.smallcase.com/blog/modern-love-indias-dating-industry/ (accessed 6 March 2024).

79 Shreya Gupta, 'Modern Love: India's Dating Industry', Small Case, 4 August 2023, https://www.smallcase.com/blog/modern-love-indias-dating-industry/ (accessed 6 March 2024).

80 'Dating Services: India', Statista, https://www.statista.com/outlook/emo/dating-services/india (accessed 20 June 2024).

81 'Dating Services: India', Statista, https://www.statista.com/outlook/emo/dating-services/india (accessed 20 June 2024).

82 Divyanshi Sharma, 'Bumble and Tinder scam on rise: Here is how you can keep yourself safe on these dating apps', *India Today*, 14 November 2023, https://www.indiatoday.in/technology/news/story/bumble-and-tinder-scam-on-rise-here-is-how-you-can-keep-yourself-safe-on-these-dating-apps-2462741-2023-11-14 (accessed 6 March 2024).

83 Anna Lovine, 'How to Stay Safe on Dating Apps', https://
    in.mashable.com/sex-dating-relationships/50687/how-
    to-stay-safe-on-dating-apps (accessed 20 June 2024).

84 'Tips for Safer Online Dating and Dating App
    Use', RAINN, https://www.rainn.org/articles/tips-
    safer-online-dating-and-dating-app-use (accessed 20
    June 2024).

Scan QR code to access the
Penguin Random House India website